to Sheilagh

who make

wort

HARD BUDGETS & SOFT STATES

Social policy choices in central and eastern Europe

by John Eatwell, Michael Ellman, Mats Karlsson, D Mario Nuti, Judith Shapiro

IPPR

INSTITUTE FOR PUBLIC POLICY RESEARCH

INSTITUTE FOR PUBLIC POLICY RESEARCH
30-32 Southampton St
London WC2E 7RA
Tel: 020 7470 6100
Fax: 020 7470 6111
postmaster@ippr.org.uk
www.ippr.org.uk
Registered charity 800065

The Institute for Public Policy Research is an independent charity whose purpose is to contribute to public understanding of social, economic and political questions through research, discussion and publication. It was established in 1988 by leading figures in the academic, business and trade-union communities to provide an alternative to the free market think tanks.

IPPR's research agenda reflects the challenges facing Britain and Europe. Current programmes cover the areas of economic and industrial policy, Europe, governmental reform, human rights, defence, social policy, the environment and media issues.

Besides its programme of research and publication, IPPR also provides a forum for political and trade union leaders, academic experts and those from business, finance, government and the media, to meet and discuss issues of common concern.

Trustees

Production & design by **EMPHASIS**
ISBN 1 86030 106 1

Contents

Preface

This is the third book that, working as a team, we have written on the economic transformation of central and eastern Europe. Since the first book, *Transformation and Integration: Shaping the Future of Central and Eastern Europe*, was published in 1995 the economic geography of Europe has changed. This is the last time, for example, that we would contemplate analysing together the problems of central Europe and the problems of Russia and the CIS. In many ways the central European countries that are candidates for entry into the European Union are approaching a 'post-transition status' – pluralistic democratic political institutions are reasonably secure, the institutions of a market economy are taking shape, and some sectors are becoming competitive. Sadly, the situation is very different in Russia and the CIS.

The economic performance of the two groups of countries is also diverging sharply. In central Europe economic stability has been attained, and growth, sometimes quite rapid growth, is underway. The CIS still suffers from monetary and financial instability and economic stagnation, even decline.

The achievements of the central European countries should not, however, be exaggerated. It is still the case, ten years after the fall of the Berlin Wall, that only Poland and Slovenia have attained the levels of income per head that they enjoyed in 1989. In these circumstances it might be supposed that consideration of social policy and of the welfare state is a luxury that must be sacrificed to the needs of transformation and growth. This is a mistake. As we will demonstrate, the welfare state makes a fundamental contribution to economic efficiency, and should be an important component of policy for a successful transition. Of course, there are levels of public expenditure that cannot be afforded. That makes the analysis of the costs and benefits of social policies all the more important. Even in the severe circumstances facing the CIS countries, well-constructed public education and health policies can make a major contribution to economic recovery.

Yet the case for the welfare state also needs to be made in western Europe. The project to modernise the welfare state, launched by Tony Blair's new Labour Party in Britain is just such a case. Confronting the economic and social problems of the 1990s and of the new century, Blair has cast the welfare state as a component of a successful employment and growth strategy, rather than solely as a means of redistributing income. The debate over the content and achievements of this modernisation is a central policy debate throughout Europe, west and east. But there is one crucial difference. Most central and eastern European countries still lack the requisite number of well-trained civil servants capable of managing the institutional and policy demands of transition – including the management of international economic relationships. Indeed, few states have either the personnel or the operational powers typical of OECD countries. In these 'soft states' the implementation of policy is a severe problem – yet it is these soft states, operating within very hard budget constraints, that must today make some very hard choices.

As in our earlier books we have benefited enormously from the advice of many colleagues, particularly those who have attended seminars on the topics covered in the book organised by the European Forum for Democracy and Solidarity. We are particularly grateful to Svetlana Stephenson of Essex University who contributed the box on homelessness in Chapter 4.

John Eatwell, Michael Ellman, Mats Karlsson,
D Mario Nuti, Judith Shapiro
December 1999

The European Forum for Democracy and Solidarity

The European Forum for Democracy and Solidarity was founded in 1993 on the initiative of the western European Social Democratic parties. The aim is to establish a close network of contacts between European parties, organisations and individuals who share Social Democratic principles and values.

The European Forum is an independent body conducted by a Steering Committee, chaired by Lena Hjelm-Wallen, deputy Prime Minister of Sweden. The forum now has offices at the Party of European Socialists in Brussels, in Budapenst and in Stockholm. The European Forum and its activities are funded by western and central European social democratic parties.

A growing number of parties, organizations and individuals all over Europe are now actively contributing to the activities of the European Forum. It involves a range of different projects, seminars, workshops, publishing the European Forum Country Updates and the Newsletter/Calendar, exchange of information and experience. One of the very first activities launched by the European Forum was to develop a programme for the economic transformation and integration of central and eastern Europe.

The active involvement and participation of many parties and individuals of central and eastern Europe has confirmed the usefulness of an independent structure. The European Forum will continue forging ties between politicians, economists and many others all over Europe who work voluntarily to strengthen democracy.

About the authors: The Forum Economic Group

John Eatwell is President of Queens' College Cambridge. He has taught economics at Cambridge since 1970, and from 1980 to 1996 was a Visiting Professor at the New School for Social Research, New York. He is on the board of the Securities and Futures Authority, and is a member of the House of Lords where, from 1993-97, he was the Labour Party's principal spokesman on economic and treasury affairs.

Michael Ellman is Professor of Economic Systems, with special reference to Transition Economics, at Amsterdam University. He has published extensively on economic systems, the Soviet and Russian economies, and transformation questions. He is a foreign member (academician) of the Russian Academy of Economic Sciences and Entrepreneurship, Fellow of the Tinbergen Institute and of NAKE, and was awarded the 1998 Kondratieff prize.

Mats Karlsson is Vice-President for External Affairs, at the World Bank. Previously, he was State Secretary for International Development Cooperation, Swedish Ministry of Foreign Affairs, 1994-99, and foreign policy adviser to the Social Democratic parliamentary group, 1991-94. He has also been Adviser to Ingvar Carlsson, co-chairman of the Commission on Global Governance, 1992-94 and chief economist, Ministry for Foreign Affairs, 1991. (The text of this book was completed prior to his joining the World Bank, and the views expressed do not necessarily represent the policies of that organisation.)

Domenico Mario Nuti is Professor of Comparative Economic Systems at the University of Rome 'La Sapienza' and (since 1993) Visiting Professor at the CIS and Middle Europe Centre, London Business School. He has been an Economic Adviser on central eastern Europe, DG-II, European Commission, Brussels (1990-1993), an Economic Adviser to the Polish Government (1994-1997) and to the Presidential Administrations of Belarus (1998) and Uzbekistan (1999), and is the author of numerous publications on post-communist economic transformations.

Judith Shapiro is Chief of the Transition Economies Section, Economic Analysis Division, of the United Nations Economic Commission for Europe in Geneva. She has contributed a number of works on health, labour, poverty and income inequality in the transition, and was formerly a resident advisor in Moscow, concentrating on analysing the links between macro-economic and social policy.

Introduction: The inclusive society and European integration

The modern economy and the welfare state

A society's attitude toward the distribution of income and well-being amongst its citizens, and especially amongst its poorest citizens, is heavily conditioned by the economic and political climate. The late 1990s have seen the culmination of a number of economic and political processes which, taken together, have produced a seismic shift in the foundations of political life in Europe:

First, the process of 'globalisation', most particularly the liberalisation of international financial markets which began in the early 1970s, has now asserted itself as a determining characteristic of economic life and hence of economic policy. Whilst the financial crises which buffeted Asia, Russia and Latin America in 1997-98 have undermined somewhat the confidence which was previously expressed in the beneficial consequences of financial liberalisation, the commitment to liberalisation by OECD governments and the international financial institutions remains. The new interest in international financial regulation sees regulation as a means, like developments in domestic regulation, of mitigating the costs of liberalisation whilst retaining the benefits.

The other major factor driving globalisation is the development of information technology and telecommunications. The full implications of these technological changes for economic and political life are still evolving. But what is clear is that they have produced an aura of rapid, destabilising, highly competitive change, which is transforming both the economy itself and also the political debate. The persistent references in modern politics to the need to 'modernise' are a response to the need (both real and imagined) to reform institutions and practices to keep pace with a changing world.

Second, there has been a steady shift in socio-economic structures and social attitudes over the past 30 years. Agriculture and industry have declined in relative importance and services have grown. Within the EU, some traditional sectors such as coal mining and textiles have almost disappeared. Most European societies have become older, and this change is set to continue for perhaps another 40 years, with profound implications for the provision of goods and services, and the funding of pensions and social security. The position of women in the family and in the labour force has changed radically, with consequent changes in the organisation of family life. In many countries both the marriage rate and the birth rate have declined.

Third, the process of European integration continues apace. The introduction of the euro will inevitably demand further institutional innovation as the policy requirements of running a single currency area become clear. Although the Maastricht Treaty apparently cast institutional relationships in statutory stone, it is to be hoped that experience will spawn reform. It was, after all, impossible to anticipate all the structures required before actually operating a totally novel monetary system. Unfortunately, treaties are typically the most inflexible frameworks within which policy might develop.

Of course, European integration goes far beyond monetary union. In addition to the ever-present problem of the Common Agricultural Policy, the development of the single market, together with the sustaining structure of social and environmental legislation, is redefining the domain of national policy-making in the member states, including the topic of this book, social policy-making.

Fourth, the welfare state is deemed to be in 'crisis'. This much discussed issue (OECD 1981, Ellman 1984) primarily reflects the 'unintended consequences' of post-war social legislation on the tax and benefit system, on the labour market and on social stratification: tax and social security legislation which generated illegal sectors, undermined national competitiveness and squeezed profits; income transfers which greatly increased the numbers in the categories targeted; the adverse effects of the large differences between the cost of labour to employers and net wages received by employees; and the emergence of a large part of the population for whom it was rational to keep out of the labour force because of the poverty trap or high 'replacement ratios' of social security to earned income. Consideration of these matters began on the right of the political spectrum, but their seriousness and the need to combat them was in due course accepted on the left as well.

Fifth, the collapse of communism and the transition toward democratic societies and market economies in central and eastern

Europe has dramatically changed the parameters of defence and security policies. The impact on economic policy is less clear. The peace dividend has generally been used to reduce fiscal deficits. The EU is committed to the widening of the Union with the accession of central and eastern European countries. But actually implementing the necessary reforms in east and west remains problematic. In part this may be because of the evident economic failure of much of the transition process up till now. No-one would have predicted in the heady days of 1989 that ten years later only Poland would have attained levels of real income per capita significantly in excess of the levels attained under communism, whilst many countries still lag behind. Political progress has, in general, been more promising. But most central and eastern European countries still lack the requisite number of well-trained civil servants capable of managing the institutional and policy demands of transition – including the management of international economic relationships[1]. Indeed, few states have either the personnel or the operational powers typical of OECD countries. In these 'soft states' the implementation of policy is a severe problem – yet it is these soft states that must today make some very hard choices.

A soft state may have large numbers of officials and adopt many laws, but its ability to formulate and implement a coherent strategy is often extremely limited as a consequence of political, financial, and administrative difficulties. In many cases the state is not a set of institutions that can ensure the efficient implementation of common goals. Instead, it is an arena in which various individuals, groups and organisations seek their own advantage. In extreme cases the state becomes a source of loot for those who are rich, powerful or well connected. Whereas west European countries such as the Netherlands, France, or the UK are capable of both adopting and implementing radical modernisation programmes, it would be a mistake to suppose that this capacity is universal. Some states cannot even pay pensions on time, or pay their employees such as teachers, doctors, or soldiers. Just collecting excise taxes on alcohol or tobacco is a difficult task in some countries.

The existence of soft states in central and eastern Europe is a transition-specific issue, deriving in part from the former interpenetration of party and state, the collapse of the party provoking a crisis of the state too. This must be taken into account in the formulation of economic and social policies.

Nonetheless, a kind of normality is becoming established in much (though not all) of central and eastern Europe. Despite the legacies of the previous 50 years, and the fact that transformation is far from complete, the choices facing much of central Europe are becoming more akin to those facing western Europe.

In marked contrast, further east, the Russian, Ukrainian and Belarus economies have deteriorated badly. The 1998 Russian default, first on its internal and then on some of its external debt, the manifest insolvency of its banking system, and the failure of the July 1998 IMF assistance package to stabilise the exchange rate and prevent the financial crisis, were major setbacks to the comfortable notion that Russia was making satisfactory progress in the transformation to a normal market economy. The failures of Russian economic policy have brought severe hardship to much of the population. Poverty is widespread. At the same time, reports that substantial sums from the central bank's foreign exchange reserves had been siphoned off to shady off-shore companies (such as FIMACO, Jersey) beyond the reach of Russian creditors and possibly used for dubious transactions; of tax collectors living off their catch; of mafia violence, political murders and the criminalisation of politics; of wages and pensions not paid for months; and of extensive corruption and capital flight, are all evidence of failure to establish a stable and attractive economic system. The dominance of the 'oligarchs' over media and politics is evidence of a transformation to a perverted 'captured' market economy. Russia, still a major nuclear power, had the worst harvest in decades in 1998 and in the autumn of that year negotiated food aid from abroad. Economic developments in that country are covered in a statistical fog. The real financial situation of all entities, from the Central Bank to the firm which 'cannot afford' to pay wages and taxes on time, is obscure. Off-budget, offshore, and non-bank (ie cash or barter) transactions are commonplace, and effective financial controls by the state or outside shareholders are conspicuous by their absence. Even the IMF, which has an office in Moscow, sends numerous missions there, regularly negotiates with the government about the details of economic policy, and has the carrot of multi-billion dollar loans to obtain accurate data, has complained about the distorted information it was given as a result of the transfer of some Central Bank assets to FIMACO. Ukraine's economy has been 'captured' by its elites, with little progress on reform. Belarus – a command economy without central planning – is in the hands of a dictator, Lukashenko, and is living off its capital.

In southeast Europe, Bulgaria, Romania and Moldova are all in serious economic difficulties. They have been unable as yet to implement consistent strategies to break out of depression and poverty.

Of Europe's post-communist failures, the wars and the atrocities in the west Balkans were perhaps the least expected. Since World War II communist, fascist and military dictatorships, and struggles between the state and terrorist organisations/armed national liberation movements (Cyprus, Basque provinces of Spain, Northern Ireland), have frequently inflicted death and suffering in Europe. But the death and destruction in the west Balkans have been of a quite different order. Murder, rape, deportation and large-scale bombing became normal political instruments. At the end of 1999 there is no permanent political solution in sight. Bosnians, Croats, Serbs and Kosovar Albanians have still to agree and accept a political conclusion to the wars in former Yugoslavia. Wounds have not yet healed.

Russia, Ukraine, Belarus, southeast Europe and the west Balkans, in their different ways, all highlight the limits of 'The New Europe' in 1999. But it must not be assumed that they are somehow a world apart from the rest of Europe. Their future rests with Europe.

Most of what we have to say in this book about social policy relates to the phase of economic reform once stabilisation has been achieved, the fundamentals of market economies have been introduced with private property and the rule of law, and when reasonably capable public institutions are established and are respected. It thus refers most directly to the situation in the five first round applicant countries to the European Union (the Czech Republic, Estonia, Hungary, Poland and Slovenia). However, much of the discussion is also relevant to the transformation issues facing eastern and southeastern Europe today. Many of the recommendations spring from lessons learnt the hard way in central Europe during the first phase of transformation.

They also derive from the experience of western Europe. There the debate over the future role of social policy has been no less fierce. The political reaction to the seismic shift referred to above led, at first, to the demise of the post-war combination of Keynesian macroeconomics and the welfare state. There was a swing toward the neo-liberalism of the

Reagan-Thatcher years (which came at an unfortunate time for the transition economies). Today the deficiencies of the neo-liberal experiment have resulted in the re-emergence of social democracy. Currently social democratic parties are involved in the government of 13 of the 15 European Union member states, a remarkable turn-around from the conservative hegemony of the late 1980s and early 1990s.

A major plank in the policy platform of contemporary social democracy has been the necessity for welfare reform. The motivation for welfare reform is complex. It derives from official and academic analysis of 'the crisis of the welfare state' and 'welfare without work', popular dissatisfaction with high tax rates and transfers to the 'undeserving', business hostility to high taxes and 'excessive' regulation, attempts by ministries of finance to attain healthy public finances, and competition between states to create attractive conditions for footloose firms and professionals in the liberalised global economy. The welfare state is not to be abolished (as in much of the neo-liberal rhetoric). It is to be *modernised*. The Blair-Schröder statement of June 1999 made this clear: 'Our aim is to modernise the welfare state, not dismantle it'. Contemporary social democracy characterises itself as applying the enduring values of the left to the problems of today, taking into account what has been achieved and recognising today's aspirations. It is applying those values on ground that has been shifted by the five components of seismic change. The new policy is claimed to recognise the failings of the old welfare state, most notably the failure to link welfare expenditure with the need to promote work. After all, the most powerful anti-poverty policy is high participation and low unemployment.

Yet contemporary social democracy has not adopted Keynesian techniques of economic management, which, in the old welfare state, were vital in providing the foundation of full employment on which the welfare state was built. The global economy of liberal capital markets is not conducive to overt macro-management, particularly the use of an activist fiscal policy. Furthermore, the welfare state is now seen as partly responsible for causing unemployment (via its unintended effects on the labour market).

It is this new political, social and economic environment that is defining the terms of the debate on social policy in both the west and the east. West and east are at very different stages of development, and hence the dimensions of social policy are quite different. Nonetheless, a common debate over the analysis of the relationship between social policy and economic performance informs policy-makers throughout Europe.

Social Democracy in the 21st century

Modern social democracy has three distinctive features. The first two were already present (to some extent) in at least some countries a decade ago (eg they had become part of the Scandinavian model in 1985-90), though they are now more strongly and decidedly asserted. The third has been strongly emphasised in some major countries more recently.

First, there is the acceptance of the primacy of markets in the direction of economic life, both domestic and international, with particular recognition of their global nature in the modern world. Thus social-democratic policies are to be implemented using market instruments instead of direct controls or the management of state enterprises. The market is part of the social organisation that is *desired*, not just a necessary means, the need for which is reluctantly admitted and which must be mastered. The new alternative is not between market and non-market. It is between a 'captured market' – captured by élites and other interest groups for their own benefit – and a well-regulated market system accompanied by welfare policies. In the latter, the regulations, institutions and policies ensure its stability, provide security for the population, and make its distributional effects more palatable. A corollary is the acceptance of the global economy as an arena in which distinct national economies are increasingly blurred and therefore domestic strategies of national economic management are increasingly constrained.

Second, gone is the commitment to public ownership and enterprise. An early step in this direction was the 1958 Bad Godesberg programme of the SPD. A later change was the repeal of the old fundamentalist clause IV of the British Labour Party Constitution in 1995. Not only has nationalisation been removed from the new agenda, but there is now a commitment to the promotion of competition, and even, where appropriate, to the continued privatisation of state assets. State regulation sets the rules of the game instead of direct interference in resource allocation. Modern social democracy recognises the potential inefficiency of state enterprises and their soft budget constraints, and the dangers of political interference in managerial appointments and in major areas of enterprise policy. Lessons have been drawn from the perceived mismanagement of western state-capitalism[2].

The *third*, novel and perhaps most important feature of modern social democracy, is its 'affordability', ie the long-term sustainability of social democratic policies without resort to the inflation tax or rising indebtedness. This is an acceptance of hard budget constraints for the state itself. Modern social democracy has recognised that Janos Kornai's 'soft budget constraint', and the negative effects that can flow from it, can be found not just in individual firms but also in the entire public sector. When inflation is used as a source of finance, it needs to rise over time in order to maintain its positive effects on economic activity and growth, and high inflation tends to hit the poorer groups of the population disproportionately hard, betraying social-democratic ideals. Rising indebtedness relative to GDP is not sustainable indefinitely, while the burden of debt inflicted on future generations also betrays social-democratic principles. Lessons have been learnt both from the demise of the earlier social-democratic model which, particularly in the recent era of low growth and high unemployment, resulted in unsustainable levels of social expenditure. In the medium term countries must live in the neighbourhood of their means, if not within their means at all times. Fiscal and budgetary discipline are necessary components of sustainable economic policies, together with appropriate monetary policies.

It is characteristic of modern social democracy that the declaration issued by Blair and Schröder in June 1999, on the eve of the elections for the European Parliament, included a section headed 'Sound public finance should be a badge of pride for social democrats'. After acknowledging the counter-cyclical role of deficits resulting from the automatic stabilisers of tax and welfare policy, and the merit of borrowing to finance investment, it was argued that:

> ...deficit spending cannot be used to overcome structural weaknesses in the economy that are a barrier to faster growth and higher employment. Social democrats also must not tolerate excessive levels of public sector debt. Increased indebtedness represents an unfair burden on future

> generations. It could have unwelcome distributive effects. Above all money spent on servicing high public sector debt is not available to be spent on other priorities, including increased investment in education, training or the transport infrastructure.

Affordability and long-term sustainability of social-democratic policies, may and often do mean cutting welfare provision, pensions, education and health. These are still regarded as good things, but should not be pursued pretending that no resource constraints arise at any level of provision. There can be too much of such good things if their provision is not sustainable. After all, the socialist agenda was always that of changing the world, not of pretending that the world is different from what it is. That you cannot have something for nothing is a corollary of affordable social democracy: citizen rights also involve obligations, workfare may have to accompany welfare.

Fleshing out the new model

With respect to earlier social-democratic projects, modern social democracy is, perhaps, weaker wine in smaller bottles. Weaker because gone are the euphoric enthusiasms for public ownership and government intervention enhancing equality and social control over economic processes. Smaller because of the more limited scale on which the newly recognised financial constraints allow the implementation of social-democratic values. Electoral victory was achieved in most of the EU countries in the late 1990s not so much by the attraction of a new project, but by the coincidental simultaneity of normal alternation in power, as well as by the crisis of the right brought about by the failure of neo-liberalism, understood as the unattractive features and global weaknesses of the Thatcher-Reagan paradigm. Modern social democracy's potential advantages of greater efficiency and of long-run sustainability were only perceivable ex-ante to a few observers. There is a significant danger that, long before its advantages will become apparent, the New Centre/Third Way[3] will be ditched by tired and impatient electorates lured by alternative populist projects. Hence the double importance of fleshing out the New Centre/Third Way with new *positive* features in addition to non-state-intervention, non-state-ownership and financial conservatism.

The intellectual basis of the New Centre/Third Way is only just being formed. Until the 1997 election New Labour's agenda was often defined in terms of a 'stakeholder economy and society' (Hutton 1995). Participation in decision-making and in national economic performance should be diffused not only among property owners but also among holders of other 'stakes', or legitimate interests, which individuals possess in their capacity as employees or consumers or simply as citizens. 'Stakeholding' replaced Blair's earlier commitment to 'communitarianism'. But after the 1997 British elections, the term was only used – or rather misused – in connection with pensions, a 'stakeholder pension' (a planned funded pension scheme for part of the population) being geared to actual individual contributions, ie to accumulated ownership rights. This is the opposite of the previous understanding of a 'stake', which by definition was distinct from, and independent of, property rights. It is no accident that the word 'stakeholder' is never used in Tony Giddens' book devoted to the Third Way (1998).

Many of the new strands of policy Giddens proposes seem to have wide appeal and are not exclusively social democratic, such as environmental reclamation and protection, or crime prevention, or the fostering of an active civil society. This does not necessarily imply that there is no longer a distinction between right and left, only that there are some areas of policy-making which have been, in part, created by the social changes of the last thirty years which the left has understood and the right has not. Some other strands explored by Giddens, which could be regarded as outside a traditional political project, are the 'democratic family' and the promotion of voluntary work.

Some positive new developments in social and economic policy have emerged from the experience of social-democratic and left wing governments:

- *The dominant weight of social-democratic governments in the EU raises the possibility of the European coordination of fiscal policies.* For the European Central Bank what should count is not the individual fiscal position of EMU members but their aggregate position. Clearly a large aggregate deficit may drive up the EMU's interest rate, interfering with the orderly conduct of ECB monetary policy. But within this aggregate constraint the fiscal stance of individual member countries will tend to affect the country risk premium rather than the basic interest rate. Fiscal stance by country could then be articulated so as to take into consideration asymmetric shocks or country-specific cyclical patterns of activity. Moreover, a proper interpretation of the Growth and Stability Pact, excluding government investment from the computation of budget deficits, would not prevent a joint European reflationary effort, through higher public investment. Public investment either takes the form of 'privatisable' assets, in which case it should be excluded from the computation of deficits, just as privatisation revenue is excluded from the computation of revenues; or it takes the form of public infrastructure that can contribute indirectly to the production of new incomes – hence the plausibility of such an interpretation.

- *Coordination of fiscal, monetary and sectoral policies of the EMU members.* At present it is unlikely that the EMU's finance ministers together with the ECB might develop into an 'economic government' for EMU, as suggested by Dominique Strauss-Kahn, the former French Finance Minister (*Financial Times*, 25 January 1999). But undoubtedly the co-ordination of economic policies within the EMU has great potential. Steps have already been taken towards the harmonisation of national statistics and the monitoring of EMU indicators.
- *A commitment to macro-economic stability.* There is something rather empty about the declaration that a politician is in favour of stability. After all, who would argue in favour of instability? Nonetheless, there is real substance to the primacy that is now attached to macro-economic discipline. On many occasions in the past, social-democratic governments have been forced to abandon their most cherished programmes in the face of macro-economic crises. The new centre left by its commitment to fiscal discipline displays a determination to prevent the same thing happening again, and hence a commitment to ensuring that social-democratic goals are attained, not just wished for.
- *The re-launch of tripartite social pacts – involving government, trade unions, and employers in order to make high and stable employment compatible with price stability.* Within the European

Monetary Union, many countries may find such pacts attractive and some international co-ordination of such pacts may be possible. The success of the Irish economy is in no small part attributable to a social pact.

- *Redistribution towards the working poor.* While the British Chancellor of the Exchequer (ie Minister of Finance) Gordon Brown has held firm to New Labour's pre-election commitment not to increase income taxes, his fiscal reforms have resulted in a substantial redistribution of income toward the poor, particularly the working poor. New Labour introduced the first general minimum wage law in the UK, and signed the Maastricht Treaty's Social Chapter. However, it also reduced benefits for some of the non-working poor.
- *Enhanced investment in education and health.* Throughout Europe the new social-democratic governments have increased social investment in education and health. There is a new emphasis both on the development of skills and on preventive medicine.
- *The implementation of family-friendly employment policies.* For example, Sweden has lengthy paid maternity leave and paid paternity leave, and publicly provided childcare, which ensure care for children, integrate fathers into families, and make it easier for mothers to combine motherhood with careers.

However, the embodiment of the New Centre/Third Way in innovative policies by the new social-democratic governments has resulted in some 'overshooting', which is itself an indication of the policy challenges faced by the New Centre/Third Way. Some examples are:

- *The proposition that the production of wealth should take precedence over its redistribution (as stated by the UK Trade and Industry Secretary Stephen Byers in February 1999).* In some policy areas there may indeed be a conflict between efficiency and redistribution, and part of that conflict may be generated by 'moral hazard', ie by opportunistic behaviour on the part of welfare state beneficiaries. However, it should not be forgotten that over a very broad area of policy there is no conflict between wealth production and its egalitarian redistribution, indeed the two may be positively correlated. Moreover, even when there is a conflict, redistribution may have the most important economic and social benefits, hard to measure but no less essential for that, and worth having: 'Unequal societies have poorer health, more violence and less self-esteem' argues Richard Wilkinson (1998; see also Glyn and Miliband 1994). Finally, a more equal society is a desirable target worth attaining even at a cost – not at any cost, but certainly at some cost.

- *The commitment to 'social inclusion' rather than 'equality'.* While social mobility is an excellent aim, especially in the sense advocated by Amartya Sen of 'enabling' policies, ie providing a socio-economic environment for the development of individual potential, it is not a perfect substitute for some degree of redistribution. Nor are the concepts of inclusion/exclusion synonyms of those of equality/inequality that they are supposed to replace. Lukes (1999) has argued that 'the newly popular language of inclusion is ideally suited for obscuring [the] division [between left and right]'. In his reflections on the Swedish old-style 'centralist and interventionist policies' of 1970-85, even Assar Lindbeck (1998) recognises that those ambitious policies to provide high income security and ample social services had not only reduced poverty and compressed the distribution of disposable income, but 'some welfare-state arrangements have also improved economic efficiency and economic growth. Various social-insurance arrangements compensate for well-known imperfections in private capital and insurance markets. Positive external (interpersonal) effects of investment in human capital mean that economic growth may be promoted by subsidies to education, and by pre-natal care and child care outside the home – at least for children from low-income families'. Lindbeck also recognises that those policies contribute to social and political stability.

- *The proposal in many countries to reduce the scope of Pay As You Go (PAYG) pension schemes and replace them with fully-funded schemes.* As will be argued below (Chapter Five) such a change has no discernible impact on macro-economic performance, and may result in a significant increase in inequality and poverty amongst pensioners, together with a considerable increase in management costs. There is no evidence to suggest that a move to fully funded, mandatory private pensions will be associated with higher savings, capital formation and growth, although it will of course bring fiscal benefits (where the PAYG scheme was financed out of taxes) or labour market benefits (where it was financed by social security contributions).

- *In some countries excessive privatisation and deregulation.* For example, new Labour has acquiesced – both before and after coming to power – in a spectacular process of demutualisation of financial institutions (building societies [ie mortgage banks], and mutual insurance companies). This has transferred capital of the order of £70 billion from social to private ownership as a result of what can only be described as a self-appropriation process by insiders on a scale reminiscent of (but much larger than) Russian privatisations. Privatisation of the British railways, realised by the Conservatives, is widely considered a failure. Privatisation of water, in both the UK and France, is not generally regarded as a great success. Deregulation of taxi fares can cause difficulties for consumers.

- *An approach to employment policies based primarily on wage restraint and labour market flexibility, and a rejection of the Keynesian interpretation of the nature of unemployment at the global level – and partially at the European level – as at least partly a demand-side problem (its likely intractability on the global or European levels purely via labour cost cuts).* In his endorsement of the US employment policy and 'culture of enterprise' (at the Milan Conference of the European Socialist Parties in early March 1999) Tony Blair did not include the (aggregate) demand-side aspects of employment policy, nor mention the fact that American labour market flexibility was just as high in 1992 when unemployment was high. The subsequent improvement in the US employment record is based (to some extent, perhaps a large extent) on straightforward Keynesian fiscal and monetary policies, consistently and persistently pursued, with low real interest rates and initially relatively large scale budget deficits leading to mounting external indebtedness,

> the counterparts of which were, initially, growing public debt, and now, growing household debt. In addition, the sustainability of the currently low level of US unemployment depends on ever-higher levels of share prices, which both permit households to build up debt and encourage foreigners to finance the US current account deficit. A sharp fall in share prices might precipitate a US recession, just as the end of the Japanese financial bubble a decade ago led to a recession in that country. Moreover, it is as implausible to regard all unemployment as structural, as it is to regard all of it as Keynesian. What kind of unemployment we have now is a complex empirical question, and highly controversial. On the basis of a survey of empirical evidence Gregg and Manning (1997) argue that the effects of labour market flexibility on employment are 'much less persuasive than is commonly believed' and that the profession's 'faith in the merits of labour market deregulation is misplaced'. Howell *et al.* (1998) and Kucera (1998) also challenge conventional wisdom; while evidence to the contrary is invoked by MacCulloch and Di Tella (1999).

Yet despite these 'overshoots', the New Centre/Third Way has restored the objectives of high participation rates and low unemployment to the centre of policy-making from which they had been expelled during the neo-liberal experiment. They are now major objectives in many EU countries, some of which often have serious problems of open unemployment and/or substantial 'welfare without work'. A large expansion of employment (measured in persons rather than hours) was the central achievement of the 'Dutch miracle' (Visser and Hemerijck 1997) in which the Dutch Labour Party and the corporatist-minded trade unions played an important role. And although many social democratic programmes are being modified in detail to accord with the new agenda, in broad outline they remain, are popular with the voters, and will continue.

Affordability of social democratic policies is a sound principle, but is not enough to sustain popular electoral support over the long run. The New Centre/Third Way is still seeking a unifying theme. The ingredients are there in the emphasis on expanding opportunities, increased participation rates, the reduction of existing inequalities, in particular those of ethnicity and gender, and a continued commitment to a decent minimum for all, equality of opportunities, security, and the provision of high quality public services.

It is against this background of the modernisation of EU social democracy, the inherited social policies and institutions, the policy advice from the international financial institutions, their – frequently difficult – fiscal situations, their current social situations, and the wishes of their peoples, that social democratic ideas about social policy in central and eastern Europe must be evaluated.

A new political economy in central and eastern Europe

In *Transformation and Integration* (Eatwell *et al* 1995) we argued that the future prosperity and security of Europe depends upon policies that transform the former communist states into socially just market economies. The future will be best served by social democratic policies: by fostering the creative power and dynamism of markets, whilst never presuming that markets are socially efficient; by equality of opportunity, because over a vast policy range equality is efficient; by dedication to social justice; by wide participation in decision making; and by identifying economic progress with sustainable development. The attainment of these goals in turn demands efficient public administration; a secure legal environment; financial stability; representative trade unions; and a structure of corporate governance that encourages growth and development in the economy.

The central and eastern European economies were typically over-industrialised and non-competitive, and needed to be transformed into economies with a modern balance between primary, secondary and tertiary sectors, *each of which must be able to compete in the world market*. Such a transformation is historically unique. However, history does suggest that economic transformation on this scale does require a developmental state, managing the appropriate mix of 'free enterprise' and public provision. Unfortunately, in the former communist countries the state was, quite understandably, seen as the problem, not the solution. It is only in recent years that the importance of the developmental state has been acknowledged. The managing director of the IMF stated in 1997, with special reference to Russia: 'No-one measured the true depth of the collapse of all administrative structures, the decomposition of the state which accompanied the collapse of the communist system.' (*Financial Times*, 10 January 1997). And with this perilously belated (and still not fully absorbed) recognition of the role of the state has also come an interest in social policy. In 1997 the World Bank devoted its annual *World Development Report* to 'The state in a changing world'. It was argued that

> An effective state is vital for the provision of the goods and services – and the rules and institutions – that allow markets to flourish and people to lead healthier, happier lives. Without it, sustainable development, economic and social is impossible... (p1)

> Low state capability in many countries of the Commonwealth of Independent States is a serious and mounting obstacle to further progress in most areas of economic and social policy (p14).

The lack of concern with social policy in the early years of transformation was understandable. The pressing demands of economic stabilisation and the recovery of output tended to overwhelm social concerns. But social policies are part of a successful transformation toward economic efficiency. They are not an 'add-on'.

In *Not 'Just Another Accession'* (Eatwell *et al* 1997) we considered the political economy of EU enlargement to the east. The treatment of enlargement as a straightforward matter of the applicant countries simply adopting the EU acquis and accepting the conditions, rules and regulations of the club, is totally inadequate due to the considerable economic problems involved. Even the most advanced central and eastern European economies have still not developed the institutional structures that are the foundations of a successful market economy. They will take decades to reach average EU levels of per capita income. For their industries as presently constituted the competitive strains of EU membership would be immense. Amongst current EU member states budgetary and institutional reforms in preparation for enlargement remain unsettled. They will have to reform the EU budget, the CAP, the structural and cohesion funds, and the EU's decision-making mechanisms. Moreover, the fear of unemployment in some member states, particularly those members with high initial unemployment and with common borders with potential new members which have much lower wage levels, can be expected to cause serious difficulties during the accession negotiations. Enlargement without dealing with these issues (of which so far only the first has been seriously tackled) risks weakening the Union.

If these issues are not better understood, the political backing for a rapid enlargement might easily evaporate, with unforeseeable consequences for the sustainability of reform in the applicant countries. Disillusionment with enlargement could open the way for political populists to wreak havoc both in applicant countries and in present member countries.

After the Commission's overall reform and enlargement plan, *Agenda 2000*, was presented in June 1997, successive EU Summits have paved the way for membership negotiations to begin. Negotiations have started with the Czech Republic, Estonia, Hungary, Poland and Slovenia. The door has now been declared open for a second wave of potential members, namely Romania, Bulgaria, Slovakia, Latvia and Lithuania to join at a later stage as long as they can meet the basic preconditions of established democratic institutions, a functioning market economy, the economic strength to compete, and acceptance of the objective of economic, political and monetary union. In all earlier EC accessions, enlargement and deepening have gone hand in hand. However, this round of enlargement to the east is accompanied by the separation of various groups of countries characterised by different degrees of exclusion.

To make an enlarged Union work, much will be demanded from present members. But nothing compares to the enormous changes required of the applicant countries. The shortcomings of transformation have created widespread resentment. Populists will seek to profit from just this sort of economic and social stress. Scapegoating has always been one of their instruments. Roma (gypsies) form a significant presence in central and eastern Europe. For centuries they have been the object of prejudice and exclusion. Vicious acts of violence have been committed against them. To take a Czech example: on different occasions Roma were thrown into rivers to drown. One of the worst populist leaders, the Republican Sládek, soon after these incidents entered the June 1998 election campaign with the words: 'Summer is coming. Time to take swimming lessons'. His party was thrown out of Parliament. But there is every reason, given Europe's history, not to take lightly the threat posed by such sentiments.

President Václav Havel, in his speech for the New Year 1999, warned: 'the walls we threw out the door in 1989 risk coming back through the window...walls against the Roma and the Germans, walls against the Russians, and the Europeans'. While hardly anyone imagines that the resentment will build up to anything like a reversal of the progress that has been made or that a 'no' majority would appear against European Union membership, populist/nationalist groups can damage the process of transformation and integration of central and eastern Europe.

Within the EU member states there is significant hostility towards enlargement. Leading right-wing populists such as Le Pen in France and Haider in Austria have sought to exploit people's concerns and fears. But few if any major parties have sought to confront the strains that may well accompany enlargement. Since the strains are often quite clear to all, whilst future gains may be less visible, enlightened and consistent political leadership on enlargement is essential.

Beyond the process of summits and formal negotiations, there is a strong case for 'confidence building measures'. In *Not 'Just Another Accession'*, we proposed an ad hoc Commission, with members drawn from both the current member states and from the applicant countries, to look at the difficult issues, express common interests and look for ways forward. Not all the answers are the subject of negotiations. So much of making the Union work involves sharing perspectives and facing future challenges with common objectives.

In this respect, social issues are of prime importance. The countries of central and eastern Europe are in the midst of the second phase of transformation. The first phase involved eliminating shortages and queues and dismantling the state-owned bureaucratically-regulated economy. The key words were stabilisation, liberalisation, and privatisation. Now those countries must determine the character of their market economy. And in doing so they need to consider the third phase of reform, taking on the full obligations of the European Union.

The initial neglect of social issues derived not just from the paramount objective of creating a basic market economy and facing up to harsh budget constraints, but also from the neo-liberal bias of much outside advice, and, importantly, the unwillingness of many 'first-generation' democratic leaders to discuss social issues at all. The common view was that there is no such thing as a *social* market economy.

They need to learn that a well worked-out social policy is not a cost to the economy, but an investment. Experience shows that equity and public investment in human development create better and stronger economies. So, strong institutions that deliver public policy, the rule of law, and sustain open societies are fundamental to the functioning of a modern economy. Yet, they have been consistently underestimated by market fundamentalists, who have frequently ignored the role of social policy in creating the necessary political basis for the market economy. Alongside sound policies and institutions, there must be a commitment to exercising responsibility for the public good. This is the foundation stone of legitimacy in democratic politics. By definition, it can never be privatised.

This is in no way a denial of the creative powers of the market economy. Indeed, it is because social democrats care about the society, that they can be better at running the market. Much of what is meant by the 'social market economy' is today mainstream policy in western Europe, part of the decent middle ground. After a period in which it seemed to be under threat the welfare state is no longer on the defensive. Reform is now the objective, not abolition. In this sense, the debates in central and eastern Europe and in western Europe are coming closer to each other. And coming close again to the historic roots of social democracy: human rights and democracy, security and equality, and social investment in education and individual empowerment. The challenge is to shape a Europe where this approach is the norm: to develop in all Europe an inclusive, empowering society.

Social policy

It is within the context of the social policy debates in the west and in the east, that we have attempted to formulate the arguments of this book. Social policy is a fundamental part of the process of transformation, both because it underpins the development of a successful economy, and because it builds the sort of society which will sustain democracy and the market economy, and which will promote the social and economic integration of Europe. That is the role that, historically, social policy has played in the development of the western European economies. It is a tragedy that the process of transformation began at a time when the dominant school of policy-makers had forgotten that lesson, and were propagating a simplistic neo-liberal approach to economic organisation (to be followed abroad if not at home). The revival of social democracy in western Europe, albeit in New Centre/Third Way garb, re-establishes the fundamental political importance in Europe of social policy, and rekindles the debate on the economic efficiency of particular social policy measures. Social policy is sometimes dismissed as an optional extra to comfort the warm-hearted. In fact it is a major ingredient of a successful economic policy.

Endnotes

1. Many of the most talented personnel have been attracted into the private sector and are proving difficult to replace.
2. More state assets have been privatised per year by Lionel Jospin in France in 1997-98 (25 billion ECU in under two years) than by Margaret Thatcher and John Major (135 billion ECU at 1998 prices in 17 years). Large-scale privatisations have been carried out or are scheduled throughout social-democratic Europe in the near future.
3. 'New Centre' is the term used by Germany's Social Democratic Party under Schroeder to describe its position. 'Third Way' is the term used by the UK Labour Party under Blair ('new Labour') to describe its position.

1. The welfare state and economic efficiency

Inequality and impoverishment

Many things have improved in central and eastern Europe as a result of the transition. Shortages and queues have generally been eliminated, the variety of goods and services available has been greatly increased, and the number of consumer durables owned by the population has increased substantially. Nevertheless, in a number of important areas, welfare has clearly worsened. This applies in particular to income distribution, poverty, participation and unemployment.

Income distribution

The measurement of income distribution raises conceptual, methodological and practical issues of a complex nature. All published income distribution data raise questions as to their coverage (part or all of the population, part or all of personal incomes), definition of 'income', unit of observation (individuals, adult equivalents, households), source (surveys, if so whose and how done, tax statistics), time period (monthly, annual, five yearly average) and the measure of inequality used. Obviously no data are perfect.

Table 1.1 provides the evidence on which a number of conclusions may be based (Milanovic 1998 Chapter 4). First, inequality increased during the early transition period in all the transition countries except Slovakia. Secondly, the increase in inequality was rapid. It seems to have been more than twice as fast as the increase in inequality in those OECD countries where inequality rose most rapidly in the 1980s (Netherlands, UK, US). Thirdly the dispersion of inequality between countries increased. Whereas before the transition their measured Gini coefficients were fairly similar, only a few years into the transition they varied enormously. Whereas some were still quite equal by west European standards (Slovakia, Hungary), some had become very unequal by west European standards (Russia, Ukraine). Fourthly, whereas in central Europe and the Balkans in 1993-95 inequality was still low or within the developed countries range, in Russia and Ukraine

Table 1.1: Inequality during the transition

	Gini coefficient[a] (annual)		
	Income per capita		*Expenditures per capita*
	1987-88	*1993-95*	*1993-95*
Central Europe			
Czech Republic	19	27	na
Hungary	21	23	27
Poland	26	28	31
Slovakia	20	19	na
Slovenia	22	25	na
Balkans			
Bulgaria	23	34	na
Romania	23	29	33
Baltics			
Estonia	23	35	31
Latvia	23	31	
Lithuania	23	37	
CIS			
Moldova	24	36[b]	na
Belarus	23	28	30
Ukraine	23	47	44
Russia	24	48[c]	50

a The Gini coefficient, which can vary between 0 and 100, compares the actual distribution of income to a perfectly equal distribution. The higher the value the more unequal the distribution. In 1995 the Gini coefficient for Denmark and Sweden was between 21 and 23; for the Netherlands, Japan and Germany 25-28; for the UK and the USA 34-36; and for Latin America about 50. According to the UNDP (1999 p21) the Gini coefficient in China in 1995 was 45.

b The UNDP (1999 p7) estimates that the Gini coefficient in Armenia in 1996 was 60, and 'a similarly high level has been reached in Moldova'. These are extremely high levels, and the comparability of the UNDP and World Bank data is uncertain.

c According to the official Russian statistics, inequality as measured by the Gini coefficient reached a peak of 41 in 1994, and has since declined, falling to 38 in 1998. These data are derived from the imperfect family budget survey and generally thought to be less reliable than the Russian Longitudinal Monitoring Survey (RLMS) that is the basis for the Milanovic estimates. The RLMS estimate of the Gini coefficient for 1996 is 49 (Mroz and Popkin 1997).

Source: Milanovic, B (1998) p41

it greatly exceeded developed country levels and was approaching Latin American levels. According to Milanovic, in 1993-95 in Russia the bottom one fifth of income recipients received less than five per cent of incomes, whereas the top fifth received 54 per cent of total income (in the UK in 1992 these figures were about seven per cent and just over 40 per cent). If the UNDP data were comparable with the World Bank data, then it would seem that inequality in some of the smaller CIS countries such as Armenia and Moldova, is even greater than in Russia and Ukraine.

There does not appear to be any reliable, internationally comparable, data on the distribution of wealth in the transition countries. It seems likely that, as is normal throughout the world, the inequality of wealth is greater than that of income.

Some increase in inequality was probably an unavoidable result of the system switch. However, the very large increases in inequality that took place in some countries (such as Russia and Ukraine) are likely to have had adverse effects on the health and self-esteem of a very large number of people and on the level of violence in society (see the Introduction).

Poverty

The available estimates of poverty are also problematic. The images they present depend on the source of the underlying data, the concept used (relative poverty, income based measures of absolute poverty, the Leiden poverty line, etc.) and the unit of observation. Milanovic's estimates, Table 1.2, are based on an absolute poverty line of four dollars (at 1990 international prices) per capita per day.

In the early transition period, poverty appears to have increased from 3 per cent to 25 per cent of the population and from

Table 1.2 Poverty during the transition

	No in poverty (%)		*Total no of poor (millions)*	
	1987-88	*1993-95*	*1987-88*	*1993-95*
Hungary	1	7	0.1	0.7
Poland	6	10	2.1	3.5
Romania	6	48	1.3	10.8
Estonia	1	34	0.02	0.5
Belarus	1	14	0.1	1.4
Ukraine	2	26	1.0	13.5
Russia	2	39	2.2	57.8
Total	2.7[a]	25.4[a]	6.82	88.2

a Unweighted arithmetic average.

Source: Milanovic, B (1998) p77.The figures for 1993-95 are based on expenditure data. The income data show higher levels of poverty but probably understate incomes. The figures for 1987-88 are based on incomes.

approximately 7 million to approximately 88 million, ie there appear to be 81 million new poor. (Nearly all the poor – 82 million or 93 per cent – live in Romania, Ukraine and Russia.) This suggests that one of the first results of the transition was to impoverish a large part of the population of the countries concerned. However, because of the sensitivity of the estimates to measurement problems, not much weight should be placed on these precise numbers. For example, if a measure of relative poverty is adopted, and poverty defined as half the official poverty linc (*prozhitochnyi minimum*), then according to official data the number of poor in Russia in 1996 would be not 57.8 million but about 15 million (Clarke, 1999). Nevertheless, the general picture of a substantial increase in poverty under transition and of a large number of people currently in poverty cannot be denied.

What were the causes of this mass impoverishment? From a statistical point of view, they were the decline in real incomes and the increase in inequality. The cake shrank, and of the smaller cake the higher income earners took a larger share. More specifically, poverty tends to be related to:

- household size and composition (in 1993 about 60 per cent of families with three or more children were poor in Russia);
- levels of education (a person with little formal education in Poland is nine times, and in Romania 50 times, as likely to be poor as a person with college education);
- sometimes to age (though pensioners have been protected in many countries); and
- employment (in Russia in 1993 63 per cent of households headed by an unemployed person were in poverty, though in Hungary, where unemployment benefits are higher, this was the case for just 17.5 per cent of such families).

This mass impoverishment is naturally distressing and undesirable from a humanitarian point of view. It has accordingly received much attention from UNICEF in its well-known series of *Regional Monitoring Reports*. It is also undesirable from the point of view of the political economy of the transition, for two reasons. First, it has reduced the demand for domestically-produced mass goods and services. In addition to competition from imports, many domestic producers have lost part or all of their domestic market because of the impoverishment of their (potential) customers. Secondly, in Russia and Ukraine it has undermined the political basis of the transition to the market and created a mass political basis for quite different policies. In Russia, new poor workers and intellectuals are an important source of support both for the CPRF (Communist Party of the Russian Federation) and for 'patriotic' political movements. Neglect of the social consequences of neo-liberalism may end up having serious consequences for all of Europe.

Participation rates and unemployment

Transition has been accompanied by a sharp decline in employment and an increase in unemployment (see Table 1.3).

Table 1.3: GDP, employment and unemployment 1990-97 (%)

	Cumulative change in: *GDP*	*Employment*	*Rate of unemployment (1996-97)*
Bulgaria	-25.2	-19.2	13.7
Czech Republic	-1.3	-5.5	5.2
Hungary	-6.2	-25.1	10.4
Poland	+11.3	-1.4	10.5
Slovak Republic	-2.0	-10.5	11.5
Russia	-40.9	-14.0	9.0

Note: Unemployment based on labour force survey data. The figure for Russia had to be estimated due to delay in conducting the labour force survey, and is probably too low. In May 1999 the officially estimated Russian unemployment rate (ILO definition) was 14.2 per cent.

Source: Commander and Tolstopiatenko (1998).

There has been a sharp decline in participation and a large increase in unemployment throughout the region (see also ILO 1996 Chapter 4). In Bulgaria, Hungary, Poland and Slovenia unemployment increased from zero to 15 per cent of the labour force within two years of the beginning of transition. In Slovakia unemployment increased from 2 per cent to 15.9 per cent in 1991 alone. In the Czech Republic measured unemployment was low in the initial transition period, but has increased significantly in 1998-99. Unemployment has been particularly high amongst ethnic minorities, the young, and the poorly educated. The growth of long-term unemployment is particularly disturbing, being around 50 per cent of the unemployed in most countries, 30 per cent in the Czech Republic. Growing unemployment has been accompanied by sharp falls in average real wages, particularly in 1990 and 1991 when statistics suggest that real wages fell by between 20 per cent and 50 per cent in most central and eastern European countries (ILO, 1996, Table 4.3).

Some decline in participation and increase in unemployment was inevitable. The sudden structural change in the economy was bound to generate unemployment, as workers shifted from the demands of a command economy to the demands of the market. Nevertheless, the scale and duration of the decline in participation and increase in unemployment indicates that in many countries transition has been a very wasteful process. The potential of a large number of now idle workers is being wasted. The transition economies have discovered that the operations of a market economy are compatible with an inefficient low-level equilibrium in which large numbers of potential workers are unable to find work.

Welfare policy and transition

The goal of creating 'efficient' economies in central and eastern Europe requires, in broad terms, the creation of economic structures that can deliver sustained increases in real living standards for the whole population. Included amongst those structures must be an 'efficient' social policy, that is a social policy which contributes to the achievement of the overall goal, especially until such time as the full benefits of the transformation have been delivered. Injustice and impoverishment turns people against the process of change. Social policy can help to create a culture of justice, honesty and fairness and provide a solid political basis for the transformation process.

The state socialist system had a developed system of welfare benefits such as pensions, child benefits, maternity leave, minimum wage, and so on. This system differed from Western welfare states in four important respects. First, it was undemocratic, reflecting what the leadership thought was desirable, rather than the wishes of the population. There was no real input into the policy process representing the beneficiaries of these programmes. Trade unions were a 'transmission belt' conveying the policies of the party-state to the workers rather than organisations conveying the wishes of the workers to the authorities. Legal NGOs did not exist. Secondly, one important aspect was the use of low prices to provide benefits to consumers. As a result there were shortages, queues, and privileged access to special facilities for the party nomenklatura. This generated a hidden inequality. These phenomena undermined the whole system and were important elements contributing to its destruction. Thirdly, the state socialist welfare system was closely linked to the production system. Most benefits were work-related. Social policy was primarily concerned with producing (and reproducing) the labour force. Thus the locus of welfare provision was the state-owned enterprises. These provided child care facilities, holiday homes, housing, health services, training, and other welfare benefits for their staff. Although this had some attractive features, in the long run it is not viable for enterprises that have to compete in open economies. Fourthly, the state socialist economic system guaranteed permanent full employment. With the transition to a democratic market economy all four of these characteristics had to change dramatically.

In the transition process, the pressure to develop efficient social policies comes from a variety of sources: the need to adapt the inherited welfare policies and programmes; the demands, needs and interests of the various social groups involved (clients, professionals, social partners, politicians); the fiscal crisis and the need to harden budget constraints; the necessity to create institutions which will sustain political stability and economic growth; the advice of the international financial institutions; and the economic and political demands of European integration. With respect to the actual experience of the past decade, useful surveys of welfare policy in the transition countries have been provided by Standing (1996) and Elster *et al* (1998, Chapter 6). Policy makers faced four broad challenges:

- to reform the education, health, pensions and housing systems inherited from the old regime (these issues are discussed in subsequent chapters of this book) so as to adapt them to democratic market economies.
- to develop policies to deal with new social problems, such as unemployment and widespread impoverishment.
- to deal with the adverse social effects of economically necessary policies, such as the divestment by enterprises of many of their

social assets and obligations.

- to take account of the advice of the international agencies, advice that was often based on inadequate analysis of the issues, and frequently had unfortunate consequences where adopted. But the agencies were often able to back their pet nostrums with large loans on soft terms.

The fiscal pressure on social policy has led to significant expenditure cuts in virtually all areas (a notable exception being health spending in the Czech Republic). Fiscal pressures have also raised demands for pension reform. This pressure is reinforced by demographic factors (though these are in general not as serious as in western Europe) and by the use of early retirement as a means of easing the pain of transition. A striking result of the impact of fiscal pressures is what has happened to the level and duration of unemployment benefits. These were often introduced at the beginning of transition with a decent replacement ratio and duration. They have since frequently been reduced, both in relative amount and in duration. As a result, in some countries the sums involved are now so small as to make registering to receive them scarcely worthwhile (which is one way, though a rather brutal one, to keep down registered unemployment).

It is important to note an aspect of social policy specific to transition countries. The transition economies have escaped from a system in which the state was the problem. The goods and services provided by the state to the general population were typically of poor quality, and not such as to engage society's admiration or affection. With this legacy, the attractions of private provision are, at least in the short run, understandable. *Re*building a public sector capable of delivering an efficient social programme is in many ways more difficult than building a welfare state from scratch.

Economic efficiency and the welfare state

Social programmes can play an important role in overcoming the waste and injustice of market economies. Empirical studies normally find that transfer payments and public provision of education, medical care and housing lead to substantial reductions in poverty and reduction in inequality. For example, Danziger, Haveman and Plotnick (1981) found that, in 1980, cash and in-kind transfer programmes reduced US poverty by about three quarters. This means that about three quarters of those who would have been in poverty without these programmes were taken out of poverty by them. In addition, they reduced the Gini coefficient by about 20 per cent – a significant reduction in inequality. However, public provision can increase inequality. This was possibly the case with housing in the planned economy (Szelenyi 1972).

Despite their potential benefits in terms of welfare and equity, it is important to pay adequate attention to the constraints on welfare programmes. Particularly important are the financial, administrative, and economic constraints.

Financial constraints

The financial vigour of the state is fundamental to the accomplishment of either financial transfers (such as unemployment benefits) or the direct provision of goods and services by the public sector (such as education or healthcare). Fiscal and monetary stability is a *pre-requisite* for the development of a coherent welfare state. There is clearly no virtue (for either public or private sectors) in unsustainable fiscal imbalance. Without proper financial controls with which a credible monetary stance is associated, all the best intentions will vanish in the gales of financial crises. Hence, given the overall macroeconomic balance, financial transfers must indeed be *transfers*, ie benefits must be paid for by taxation or social security contributions. Similarly, the direct provision of goods and services must be paid for, either by the recipients directly, or, if provision incorporates some element of redistribution (housing provided below cost, health care provided free or cheaply, education provided free or cheaply) then by taxation. To some extent borrowing 'automatically' finances consumption during cyclical downturns, as tax revenues fall and welfare spending (particularly unemployment compensation) rises. But this automatic stabiliser (or 'dampener') should be a cyclical phenomenon, with upswings roughly balancing downswings. Permanently financing consumption (via transfers or below cost provision) by borrowing is a recipe for eventual financial disaster. An efficient system for the collection of tax revenues, and for administration of the public finances, is a necessary precondition of the attainment of the desirable goals of a welfare state.

An important aspect of any efficient tax system is that it should be broadly accepted as fair. The burden should fall on those who can afford it, but should not reach what are generally considered to be absurdly high levels on anyone. If they are not broadly accepted as fair, then taxes may prove very difficult to collect. The shift in western European economies from high marginal rates of income tax to broad based consumption taxes and 'sin taxes' (tobacco, alcohol, pollution) has been in part motivated by social antipathy toward high marginal rates, even by those who are never likely to pay them. Equally, governments must also try to show that they can be relied upon to spend taxpayers' money efficiently, so that the taxes paid are not squandered, but provide obvious benefits.

So all the discussion of the welfare state that follows must be carefully qualified with respect to the maintenance of financial stability. Ambitious social welfare plans are only feasible (let alone efficient) if they can be paid for – and paid for without reliance on the manifestly inegalitarian inflation tax. The fiscal pressures that are in evidence in central and eastern Europe will necessarily place tight constraints on the development of the welfare state. A rigorous assessment of the value of welfare spending to society as a whole is required.

Administrative constraints

Social programmes require an effective administration that can levy taxes and administer the programmes efficiently. One of the reasons why the Russian PAYG pension system operates so badly is that this condition is not met. Much economic activity escapes paying pension contributions, and part of the contributions that are paid are diverted to other uses or even stolen by officials at all levels. Hence pensions are frequently not paid on time. This is another example of that most unfortunate part of the neo-liberal euphoria of the early transition period: far too little attention was given to maintaining the administrative capacity of the state (Eatwell *et al* 1995 Chapter 2).

As a result governments have great difficulties in actually implementing reforms, even when they have been formulated and accepted by the political process. As Elster *et al* (1998 pp 233-234) have quite rightly observed:

To launch reforms, political actors have to be 'strong' enough to carry out their policy intentions. 'Strength' means, first of all, that post-communist coalition governments must have the ability to reconcile conflicting interests and actually come to a decision. On the contrary, political instability invites political actors to adopt short-term, 'trial-and-error' policies. Unfortunately, it is the latter scenario that has become the reality in most post-communist societies. Adding to political instability, post-communist governments do not usually possess sufficient financial and administrative resources to implement policies. Moreover, governments still lack strong, reliable societal partners, organised interests outside the realm of the parliamentary system, which could be used to overcome resistance, launch reforms, and assume welfare responsibilities. Only the Czech reformers have enjoyed more favourable conditions which enabled them to implement a number of far-reaching and probably irreversible changes in the welfare state.

Economic constraints

The process of transition demands high levels of investment to make up for the inappropriate capacity inherited from the past. This involves not only investment in new industrial capacity and infrastructure but also investment in people. Whilst some aspects of the welfare state are geared toward improving levels of consumption (pensions, housing), others are an investment in the quality of the labour force. In this respect not only are education and basic healthcare clearly investments, but so are those measures designed to secure decent standards of living, especially for children. Poverty and inequality are detrimental to (potential) economic growth both because of the physical and psychological deterioration of the labour force, and because of the waste of those who have no opportunity to develop their talents.

But the return on the resources devoted to the welfare state is medium to long term, and is not immediately identifiable in a profit and loss account. Moreover, the diversion of resources to the welfare state may have immediate damaging consequences on performance elsewhere in the economy. A difficult balance must be struck. That requires not only consideration of the costs of the welfare state, but also recognition of the benefits of the contribution of the welfare state to economic efficiency.

Equity and efficiency: an introduction

Social policy has two dimensions: the transfer of income to those in need through tax and benefit systems, and the direct provision of goods and services by the public sector. The first dimension includes unemployment benefits, sickness and invalidity benefits, benefits for children and the retired, and so on. The second dimension includes the public provision of health care, education and public housing. The public provision of pensions embodies both dimensions. Basic state pensions are often an important means of distributing 'safety-net' financial benefits to the elderly, whilst state pension systems can provide a vital financial service for all sections of the population. Financial transfers and direct provision of goods and services are typically combined within the definition of 'the Welfare State' because the provision of goods and services by the state typically (though not invariably) incorporates decisions about the distribution of those goods and services amongst the population – state provision is often significantly more egalitarian than market provision. Many of the issues now being confronted by policy-makers in the transition economies are also matters of current debate in western economies (see, for example, Commission on Social Justice, 1994). What has become clear in the western debate is that, as economic and social circumstances change, the form and content of an efficient welfare state must change with them.

The economic analysis of the 'value of welfare spending' has frequently been presented as a relationship between 'equity' and 'efficiency'. The term equity is ambiguous. On the one hand, it may be associated with equality (either equality of opportunity or equality of outcome, or some mixture of both). On the other hand, it may simply mean 'fair', as in individuals being treated in an equitable manner. For the purposes of the discussion that follows, the term is used simply as an omnibus term for the egalitarian objectives of social welfare programmes. All such programmes, whether transfers or direct provision, seek to achieve a distribution of well-being which is different from that which the market would achieve without such intervention. It is this later aspect of the welfare state that lies behind the long-standing economic policy debate on the relationship between 'equity' and 'efficiency' – what are the consequences of 'interfering' with the market?

The proposition that efficiency demands the abandonment of equity was famously argued by Arthur Okun in his book *Equality and Efficiency: The Big Trade-Off*. He maintained that in market economies inequalities in living standards and material wealth

> reflect a system of rewards and penalties that is intended to encourage effort and channel it into socially productive activity. To the extent that the system succeeds, it generates an efficient economy. But that pursuit of efficiency *necessarily* creates inequalities. And hence society faces a trade-off between equality and efficiency (Okun, 1975, p1, emphasis added).

The core argument of Okun's book has been widely accepted, not only amongst social commentators of a more conservative or free-market persuasion, but also on the social-democratic left. Among this latter group support for greater egalitarianism, and for socially redistributive policies, often derives, as Okun himself suggests, from a desire to 'put some humanity into efficiency' (Okun, 1975, p120). In other words, redistributive policies may be considered to be socially desirable even though it may at the same time be conceded reluctantly that they reduce economic efficiency. From this perspective, the case for the welfare state is social and political, not economic. Equity, it is argued, is the enemy of efficiency.

In direct contrast, Nicholas Barr (1992, 1998) has argued that the welfare state can and should contribute to economic efficiency:

> The welfare state is much more than a safety net; it is justified not simply by any redistributive aims one may (or may not) have, but because it does things which private markets for technical reasons either would not do at all, or would do inefficiently. We need a welfare state of some sort for efficiency reasons, and would continue to do so even if all distributional problems had been solved. (Barr, 1998 p409).

Barr makes clear that there are two questions to be confronted in considering whether there is indeed a trade-off between efficiency and equity:

- First, whether direct interference in the market-determined distribution of income, say by taxes and social transfers, diminishes efficiency. This question does not necessarily have a unique answer. It requires, for example, consideration of whether the impact on efficiency is affected by the *scale* of interference.
- Second, whether goods and services, including financial services such as pensions, would be most efficiently provided through the state. This includes whether the state should produce the goods and services itself, or whether it should purchase them from the private sector.

Initially, the search for competitive efficiency in the transition economies of central and eastern Europe took place within an environment of sharp cumulative falls in national output, high rates of inflation and the consequent pains of anti-inflation policies, high levels of hidden employment and inactivity, and severe fiscal pressure. Whilst in some countries output is now up and inflation is low, in many countries adverse conditions still prevail. In such circumstances there are pressures on all forms of social spending, and it may seem that the overriding imperative is 'to get the economy working' and that social policy is a luxury only to be enjoyed in the future when times are better. But, as is increasingly recognised, sustained economic growth depends as much on building social capital in the form of institutions that promote social cohesion, as it does on harnessing the creative power of markets. Hence even in these difficult circumstances social policy is an important component of the search for economic efficiency. Moreover, whilst it is obvious that the transition economies cannot in the short to medium term emulate the welfare policies of west European countries, those which aspire to membership of the European Union will need to work toward at least those aspects of the social market economy which are required by the *acquis communautaire*.

The analytical background to the debate over the relationship between equity and efficiency is sketched out in the box below.

Equity and efficiency: trade-off, watering can, or positive-sum game?

Okun's argument that there is a 'great trade-off' between equity and efficiency is commonly believed to be supported by core arguments of orthodox economic theory. Starting from the premise that an unfettered market distributes resources efficiently, orthodox theory suggests that interference with market signals, whether by administering or altering prices (say by a minimum wage, or by rent control), or by means of revenue-raising taxes to pay for social provision, will undermine that efficiency. Moreover, the direct provision of goods and services by the state is likely to be inefficient because it is not subject to the rigours of market discipline.

Closer examination reveals that the argument is not as powerful as it might at first appear. It is difficult to assess the social value of any interference with the price mechanism which itself results in a significant alteration in the distribution of income. Only those changes that have no impact on the distribution of income (and there are virtually none of those) stand any chance of simple evaluation. The difficulties are revealed by the fact that the definition of social efficiency in orthodox economic theory, the concept of Pareto Optimality[3], says nothing whatsoever about the distribution of income. A Pareto Optimum is simply a position of the economy in which no one individual can be made better off without some other person being made worse off. All inter-personal comparisons of the scale of gain and loss are deliberately eschewed. The reason for this is that according to traditional economics it is simply impossible to say whether, if you are forced to give me $1, your loss in well-being is balanced by my gain. If you are rich, you may not care about a $1 foregone. If I am poor it may matter very much to me. But exactly what the balance of gain and loss might be is outside the calculus of traditional orthodox economics. Hence, economists have traditionally eschewed the comparison. Any change in economic conditions that results in a deterioration in the circumstances of any individual, regardless of that individual's initial well-being, lies outside the Paretian criterion of efficiency, and no judgement can be made using this criterion[4]. Hence a famine in which the starving can only be provided with food by taxing the well-off may be 'Pareto-efficient' even if non-economists regard it as outrageous and immoral.

Then why bother with this minimalist definition of efficiency? The strength of the Pareto criterion derives from its association with what is called the Fundamental Theorem of Welfare Economics. The first part of that theorem states that if the economy is in a perfectly competitive equilibrium, then it is Pareto efficient. A powerful link is thereby established between an idealised market economy, and a definition, however limited it may be, of efficiency[5].

It is important to note that despite the impression often created by economics textbooks, it is methodologically unsound to jump to strong policy conclusions from extremely simplified models. It is logically first of all necessary to demonstrate that they capture the essential aspects of the problem concerned so that conclusions valid in the model are also valid in the real world. Moreover, many simple models of the market economy presented in economics textbooks, which are interpreted to show the benefits of laissez faire, in fact simply show that trade can be mutually beneficial. This is true, important, and for many people counter-intuitive. It is, however, a somewhat limited proposition.

Furthermore, the argument rests on there being 'perfect' markets[6]. For example, an impoverished child should be able to borrow sufficient funds in a perfect capital market to buy the most expensive education, in the confident expectation of a stream of lifetime income that would make the investment worthwhile. Once it is admitted that markets are not perfect then there are major problems that vitiate the relevance and applicability of most standard welfare theorems. It is then difficult to argue on purely theoretical grounds that the 'disturbance' of relative prices by taxes and welfare payments is damaging economic optimality. As the theory of the second best long ago pointed out, in a non-optimal economy, it does not necessarily follow that market-friendly reforms will raise efficiency.

It also assumes that all goods are private goods and that there are no public goods.[7] Since it is not possible to cover the cost of public goods by user charges, the market will underproduce them, as Adam Smith pointed out.

Given all these qualifications, it is not surprising that empirical work has tended to identify relationships between equity and efficiency which are quite different from those which orthodox theory would predict. A well known and very well informed, but by now somewhat dated, review of much of the empirical literature, especially focusing on the effect of US programmes, can be found in Danziger, Haveman & Plotnick (1981). Corry and Glyn (1994) summarise similar work that has also been done on the worldwide relationship between equity and growth:

> Alesina and Rodrick (1992) relate average growth rates for 65 countries over the period 1960-85 to income inequality at around the start of the period. After allowing for other influences such as the initial level of productivity, they found that the higher the share of top incomes...the significantly lower is growth, whilst higher shares for the poor and especially the middle-income groups are associated with higher growth. They conclude that 'countries where income is more equally distributed also grow faster'. Persson and Tabellini (1992) reach essentially the same conclusion.
>
> Such analysis has...received the endorsement of the World Bank... Their *World Development Report* 1991, noted that 'there is no evidence that saving is positively related to income inequality or that income inequality leads to higher growth. If anything, it seems that inequality is associated with slower growth'...
>
> a study by Garrison and Lee (1992) of the impact of taxation across 65 countries...concludes that 'cross-country evidence provides no support for the supply side hypothesis that increases in tax rates adversely affect economic activity.'

On the basis of a cross-country study explicitly aimed at assessing the impact of the welfare state on growth of output per head Walter Korpi concluded:

> The cross-sectional and over-time analyses performed here give no indication that increases in the size of public sectors, expanding welfare state programs, lower income inequality, or higher potential for political and organizational penetration into markets have been negatively associated with product and productivity growth in the 17 'core' capitalist democracies during the period 1950-1973. (Korpi, 1985, p112).

Similarly, he found no negative relationship between a pre-existing welfare state and growth in the period 1973-79. Accordingly, Korpi sees social policy as an irrigation system that stimulates human capital formation and economic growth. People who benefit from adequate medical care and nutrition as babies, and adequate housing and education as children and young adults, have a good chance of turning into productive members of society. Clearly this metaphor throws some light on the development of the advanced welfare states in the post-World War II period.

However, experience of many welfare states has shown that there really can be significant trade-offs (Esping-Anderson, 1996). Germany has traded off employment for income with its generous 'welfare without work' policies. The Netherlands has traded off equality for employment and generated the 'polder miracle' and Sweden has traded off skill augmentation and additional work for equality of outcomes. The US has traded off high wages for employment creation. It is because of the increased consciousness and visibility of these trade-offs that attention has increasingly switched in political and policy discussions to the search for positive-sum solutions, that is for policies that generate an increase both in efficiency and in equity. What such policies are there? According to Esping-Andersen (1996, p264):

> The most logical solution that presents itself is that we rethink the idea of redistribution and rights: accepting inequalities for some, here and now, but guaranteeing at the same time that those who fare less well 'here and now' will not always do so; that underprivilege will not be a permanent fixture of anyone's life course. This kind of dynamic, life-chances commitment to equality is arguably a positive-sum solution in that it stresses a social policy more explicitly designed to optimise the self-reliant capacities of the citizenry. Again, the core of such a model's social citizenship guarantees would combine education and proactive income maintenance [ie income maintenance that is related to work].

It is clear that measures that enforced total equality of outcome, whatever the input by the individual, would rob society of any incentives to work, compete or innovate. There is a balance to be struck. Equality of opportunity is clearly important in defining the prior conditions for economic efficiency. Resources should therefore be distributed in such a manner that individuals have reasonable equality of opportunity. That must necessarily mean that income differentials are not excessive, since opportunity is often linked to income. Yet redistribution should not be so severe as to remove all incentives. Moreover, redistribution should work with the market. For example, it is foolish to introduce large, means-tested benefits for the unemployed, which produce a situation in which going out to work and earn can actually reduce a family's real income. Benefits should be structured in such a way that work increases real income. Similarly, if there is an active private market in housing, the use of rent controls to protect the poor may well result in inadequate provision. Far better to protect the poor from exploitation by the social provision of affordable housing.

The equity and efficiency debate does not only involve the question of redistributing income by means of taxes and monetary benefits, it also extends into the consideration of which goods and services should be provided by the state, and which by the market, and to what extent the state should regulate markets.

The economics of information provides a new insight into that problem (see Barr, 1992). Where accurate information is readily available, competitive markets may work reasonably well. But where information is not readily available, or where production and/or distribution are monopolised, then markets may be very inefficient. It also matters whether bad choices *matter*. If bad choices lock individuals or society into bad decisions for substantial periods of time then markets may be inefficient. If mistakes are easily redressed then markets may work well. Thus, as Barr points out, in general the provision of food is best left to the market, once suitable steps have been taken to provide the public with the information they need to make informed choices. The same is true of most consumer goods, though regulation may be necessary in cases in which the public has greater difficulty in acquiring the information it needs. Food hygiene standards are an example. But where information is scarce and complex, markets may be highly inefficient. An example is health care, where not only is the consumer almost inevitably badly informed, but also he or she does not even know how much healthcare they are likely to need. In this case markets, including insurance markets, are likely to be highly inefficient.

Another dimension is provided by interdependence in consumption and production – what economists call 'externalities'. For example, it has little effect on your well-being whether or not your neighbour goes on a diet. However, your well-being may be considerably endangered if your neighbour does not have access to reasonable healthcare and as a result develops a contagious disease.

The argument can best be summed up as follows:

- The welfare state, by means of transfers or direct provision of goods and services, is essentially a system of social insurance, in which society pools risks which, due to lack of information or markets, are not susceptible to individual insurance. In this respect it enhances the efficiency of the economy.

- But because the welfare state operates outside immediate market disciplines it is itself susceptible to inefficiency, and may have adverse effects on incentives. It is therefore important to work with the grain of the market where possible, and where this is not possible to regularly monitor the impact of welfare state measures.

- There is therefore no simple 'big trade-off'. Indeed equity is, in many circumstances, positively related to efficiency. Welfare state measures may function as an irrigation system, enhancing efficiency. There is a complex balance to be found between the enhanced efficiency that can derive from welfare state measures, and the diminution of efficiency that can arise through the resulting price distortions, high tax rates and reduced work incentives. There is a general need to find positive sum policies which increase both efficiency and equity. This is the core of the current debate about modernising the welfare state.

- An important externality produced by the welfare state is the development of social cohesion and trust.

The welfare state and employment

In the post-World War II period, it was widely assumed that the welfare state, by redistributing from high savers to high spenders raised effective demand and hence contributed to full employment. In addition, the automatic stabilisers provided by the tax and social security system were thought to dampen fluctuations and thus reduce cyclical unemployment. Furthermore Swedish-style growth of employment in publicly provided services (such as childcare) clearly helped raise participation rates.

Experience with the welfare state showed, however, that the welfare state can reduce both the supply of labour and the demand for it. It can reduce the supply of labour by providing transfer payments that are attractive relative to work (Danziger, Haveman & Plotnick 1981, Haveman 1985). It can reduce the demand for labour if firms are unable to pass on social insurance contributions to their customers so that they fall on profits. This seems to have been the case in the 1980s in some small open economies (eg Netherlands and Sweden) where prices in the tradeables sector are largely set by international competition. Hence modernisation of the welfare state began in these countries and only later spread to the major EU countries.

In those EU countries where neo-liberals came to power (eg the UK under Thatcher) substantial cuts in welfare state programmes were undertaken for political reasons and Keynesianism was abandoned. As defenders of the welfare state correctly anticipated, this led to unemployment levels unprecedented in the UK's post second world war experience.

These experiences illustrated the important fact that both welfare state policies and anti-welfare state policies can generate unemployment.

In recent years much attention has been given to the contrast in employment experience between the EU and the US. The differences in the performance of the US and EU labour markets in the past decade may be summarised as:

- Europe has higher unemployment and has failed to generate new jobs on the scale of the US.
- Europe has far more long-term unemployed. In Britain and western Germany 35 per cent of the unemployed have been out of work for more than a year; in the US only 11 per cent. Europe has relatively low inflows to the pool of unemployment, but long unemployment duration; the US has high inflows, but much shorter unemployment duration.
- The US has lower relative pay than Europe. In the US one quarter of full-time workers earn less than two thirds of the median wage. In the EU only one fifth of full-time workers have earnings that low. Over the past decade real wages for the lowest paid workers have grown by 2.5 per cent per year in western Germany (1983-90), by one per cent per year in Britain (1980-92), but have *fallen* by 1.2 per cent per year in the US.
- In the US unemployment benefit is substantially lower than in Europe, and eligibility is far more restricted. The average replacement ratio is just under ten per cent in the US, a little over 20 per cent in Britain (though this is being reduced) and 30 per cent in Germany.

The orthodox interpretation of this combination of circumstances is that the American labour market is more flexible, less regulated and therefore 'more efficient' than the European labour market, and that it is this flexibility which has ensured that America has not suffered the very high rates of unemployment now common in the EU.

However, in order to consider the effect of economic institutions and economic policy on unemployment, one has to eliminate the effect of other factors that influence unemployment. Two such factors are the demographic situation and penal policies.

In the US, there are structural differences in unemployment rates between demographic groups. Unemployment is higher among the young, for example, than among people in their thirties and forties. Hence the entry of the baby boom generation into the labour market and its subsequent ageing, automatically had significant consequences for the aggregate unemployment rate. Shimer (1998) estimated that the entry of the baby boom generation into the labour market in the 1960s and 1970s raised the aggregate unemployment rate by about two percentage points. The subsequent aging of the baby boomers had reduced it by one and a half percentage points.

As far as penal policy is concerned, Richard Freeman has pointed out that low US long-term rates of unemployment are influenced by the very high level of imprisonment in the US:

> In 1993, 1.9 per cent as many men were incarcerated as were in the labour force and 4.7 per cent as many were on probation or parole, so that 6.6 per cent as many were under the supervision of the criminal justice system as were in the work-force. Of those incarcerated, two-thirds were in state or federal prisons and thus comparable in terms of length of stay out of the job market to the long-term unemployed. Imprisonment in Europe is one-tenth as great. The growth of prisoners in the US during the 1980s was nearly nine per cent per year and the growth rate shows no sign of slackening. At current rates, in the year 2000 the US will have a larger share of its male work-force imprisoned or long-term unemployed than Europe will havc long-term unemployed on the dole. (Freeman, 1995).

In addition, many of the newly created jobs in the US have been in low paid service occupations. Indeed, the pay of many of thcm is so far below the US average, that one can raise the question of whoether they are really ‘employment’ at all.

In 1937 Joan Robinson pointed out that in circumstances in which those who lose their jobs have no other source of income (ie support from the welfare state is low or non-existent) the unemployed have to find some way of scraping together a living, typically in low paid services. Her example was someone selling matches in the street. If those who cannot find employment in the high productivity sector of the economy do find some way of scraping by in low productivity employment, then typically they will be recorded in national statistics as being employed[1]. This is why in many relatively poor countries with very little, if any, unemployment pay, recorded unemployment is often very low. For example, today, one of the OECD countries with the lowest rate of *recorded* unemployment is Mexico.

Joan Robinson did not consider scraping by in advanced economies to be employment. For her employment involved being engaged in a category of job that would be offered when the economy is working at full capacity. Instead, she characterised 'scraping by' as 'disguised unemployment'. Disguised unemployment is defined as individuals performing tasks with a level of productivity below that which they could attain if the level of demand in the economy were such as to sustain full employment. An increase in demand would accordingly lead to them transferring to higher productivity activities. Output would increase without any increase in employment. Similarly, a fall in demand would be accompanied by relatively small decline in employment as workers transfer into disguised unemployment. Despite the fact that those who are scraping by are counted amongst the employed, disguised unemployment will tend to have dynamic disadvantages similar to those associated with long-term unemployment, such as the erosion of skills.

Some employment in the United States, particularly employment in low-productivity services accords with Joan Robinson's definition of disguised unemployment. Not only is social security provision much lower than in Europe, but also overall productivity growth in the economy is very low, around half the European average (see Table 1.4).

However, productivity growth in those sectors that are exposed to international competition, such as manufacturing industry, is equal to,

Table 1.4 Overall productivity growth, GDP per person employed

	1961-70	*1979-90*	*1991-96*
France	5.0	2.2	1.2
West Germany	4.3	1.4	1.7
Italy	6.2	1.7	2.0
UK	3.3	1.7	2.1
US	2.3	0.6	1.1

Note: the later figure for West Germany is for 1991-94.

Sources: European Economy, Annual Economic Reports; OECD National Accounts, 1979-1991.OECD Statistical Compendium 1997.

or higher than the rate in Europe. These facts suggest that the US economy may have a dual structure: an advanced, high productivity sector, and a backward sector with very low productivity growth which acts as a 'sponge', soaking up the unemployed. In Japan very low productivity, highly protected, agricultural and service sectors perform a similar function. Calculation of rates of disguised unemployment in the G7 economies in the 1980s suggest that 'true' unemployment (that is measured *plus* disguised) in the US and Japan exceeded 'true' unemployment in France and Germany (Eatwell 1997).

If, due to the disruption of transition, depression, or low growth, the number of jobs available in high productivity sectors is less than the number of people looking for work, then high levels of employment in low productivity sectors may well be efficient by comparison with large numbers of workers being supported in idleness. In particular, low paid jobs may be useful for the young or for immigrants, making their first step up the employment ladder. The crucial question for economic policy is whether these jobs really do provide an initial step up a ladder that will take their occupants to well paid jobs in a few years, or whether they trap their occupants in a ghetto of low pay. Initial research (Esping-Andersen 1996 p17) suggests that in the US opportunities for upward mobility are substantial, but *conditional upon adequate skills*. Unskilled workers have a high probability of being confined to a low wage ghetto. Hence preventing the emergence of a proletariat of the working poor requires the provision of adequate training facilities or the provision of public sector employment.

Employment and social policy

More generally, an important lesson to learn from the experience of the OECD countries is that employment policies should both enhance flexibility by investing in skills and in efficient structures of industrial relations, and should strive to attain sustainable rates of growth consistent with high levels of employment. Indeed, labour market flexibility is often preceded by high rates of investment and growth. It may also be enhanced by social pacts encompassing working practices and wages. The large falls in unemployment in Poland have been associated with a tripartite agreement that regulated wages growth.

Flexibility without growth will make significant inroads into unemployment only to the extent that people are forced into low-productivity jobs. Growth without flexibility will encounter inflation constraints whilst unemployment remains high.

Any employment policy in the transition economies will need to confront the problem of a chronic lack of new competitive industries. At present the transition economies do not possess enough competitive capacity to produce the goods and services for the home and foreign markets which would allow them to sustain a high employment level of demand, or anything like it. This is an important part of their employment problem *and* their social welfare problem: not enough competitive capacity. And most important of all, there are not enough people with the skills, including managerial skills, to compete in the modern global economy, and the opportunity to use those skills with the latest techniques, producing the latest products. It is skills and the social and economic framework within which those skills can be deployed effectively that really matter. In a global economy where techniques and capital are more mobile than ever, and markets are truly international, what distinguishes a national economy are the skills and talents of its people and the efficiency of its institutions. If skills and talents – everything from management techniques, to handicrafts, to computer sciences, to electrical engineering, to design – are neglected then a country first loses its competitive edge, and then slips into a decline characterised by growing trend unemployment.

The collection of essays edited by Glyn and Miliband (1994) indicates that strongly egalitarian policies in education and training (including adequate funding for those undertaking education and training) are necessary components of the high rate of accumulation of skills necessary to compete, and of the 'labour market flexibility' which high levels of education and training bring in their wake. It is particularly clear that an inegalitarian educational system[2] is likely to prove incapable of matching the achievements of a more egalitarian, less market driven system (Edwards and White, 1994).

An efficient welfare state

As far as employment is concerned, there is clearly a mutually reinforcing relationship between equity and efficiency. Fully-employed economies will tend to be more equal economies. Full employment being typically associated with higher rates of growth, a more equal economy is likely to result in long-term gains in real income for individuals throughout the income distribution. But these gains are only possible within a wide-ranging institutional framework best characterised as a mixed, social market economy. That sort of framework has the record of achieving greater equity and efficiency.

Yet to adopt the simplistic proposition that there is *never* any trade-off between equity and efficiency would be absurd. In a mixed, social market economy, it is important that where possible social measures should work with the grain of the market. That may involve acceptance of outcomes that are not egalitarian. The best way to proceed is to adopt a clear set of social goals (growth, employment, decent levels of nutrition, health, education, housing, and so on) and strive to achieve those goals within the context of transition. There are of course likely to be trade-offs between those goals, and difficult choices must be made. To make those choices, there must be a clear appreciation of the contribution of the welfare state to economic efficiency, and the size of welfare state that is appropriate to the stage reached in the transition. A welfare state can be an integral component of the construction of an efficient market economy.

So whilst the idea that there is a simple trade-off between equity and efficiency is simply wrong, it is equally wrong to deny that inequality may in some circumstances be the inevitable product of efficient markets. A balance is required. The balance to be achieved is between

- the redistribution which underpins human dignity and equality of opportunity,
- the pursuit of high participation and low unemployment, and
- the dynamism of the market economy.

Achieving the balance appropriate to the stage of transition is the fundamental task of social policy in the transition economies.

One further important component of a well-balanced policy will be the requirement that the operations of the welfare state are themselves efficiently organised. This poses rather different challenges to the two dimensions of the welfare state: on the one hand financial transfers; and on the other hand the direct provision of goods and services.

Targeting financial transfers

The design of efficient financial transfer policies (income support, poverty relief, child support, and so on) poses a number of difficult problems. Given the tight fiscal constraints under which the transition economies are operating, there is a clear incentive to attempt to target transfers as accurately as possible. Unfortunately targeting can be highly inefficient:

- First, means-tested benefits tend to create a poverty trap, since the withdrawal of benefit as incomes rise imposes a very high marginal rate of effective tax on some of the poorest sections of society.
- Second, targeting creates a clear incentive for fraud, as individuals attempt to suggest that they are part of the targeted population, when in fact they are not. The perception of widespread fraud undermines society's commitment to all aspects of the welfare state.
- Third, targeting is very expensive to administer. The costs of identifying the target population, minimising fraud, and distributing a targeted benefit can be extremely high and may well exceed the losses implicit in un-targeted distribution.
- Fourth, some of the target group may not receive benefit because targeting policy stigmatises the benefits, and therefore some intended beneficiaries do not apply.

Targeted benefits therefore tend to be most efficient when: (a) targeting is not based on a means test, or (b) the benefit is relatively small compared to potential income, or (c) the targeted population is easy to identify, children, for example, or the blind, or (d) the targeted population is a relatively small proportion of the population as a whole. Where these conditions do not apply, the transactions cost of supplying targeted benefits may well be very high indeed and instead of saving money, the attempt to target benefits may result in substantial waste.

World Bank economists tend to argue that Russian social policy is inefficient, since a high proportion of benefits go to the non-poor. But as Clarke (1999) has pointed out, this is very misleading. The reason for this situation is that pensions are the largest item of transfer payments and pensions are still sufficient to keep most pensioners above the (low) poverty line. Hence the fact that most transfer payments are paid to the non-poor simply shows how effective transfer payments can be in keeping people out of poverty.

Direct supply

The argument for the direct supply of goods and services by the state has been made above in terms of the economics of information: where individuals lack information or the ability to use information effectively, where production is monopolised and where decisions may have very high costs, the market may be very inefficient. In these circumstances regulation (as in food hygiene), state purchases from the private sector (the building of public sector housing), or the direct provision of goods and services (healthcare) may be more efficient.

The state may also be a more efficient provider where large economies of scale are involved. This is the case, for example, in the provision of basic pensions. State provision of pensions is essentially a system of social insurance – we insure against the possibility of living long without income. Involving the whole society in bearing that risk not only spreads risk most widely, but also significantly reduces transaction costs. The provision of pensions by a number of private companies can involve duplicated actuarial analysis and heavy costs of management and sales, together with the need to pay dividends to shareholders. Public provision is also the only effective way to 'insure' against inflationary episodes or stock market crashes disrupting pensions.

The direct supply of goods and services by the state should be efficient, and take the needs and desires of the people fully into account. Central planning failed on both counts. It is important that the provision of goods and services by the state in transition economies should not repeat those failings. In a democracy the direct provision of goods and services must be seen to be fair, and must take account of the needs and aspirations of the people. Hence the provision of goods and services by the state should be subject to regular audit, with careful comparisons being made with public provision in other countries, and provision by the private sector. In making comparisons, full account should be taken of all costs, including costs of administration and other transaction costs. There should be no ideological predisposition toward public or private provision. It is the efficient attainment of social and economic goals that matters.

Securing support for the welfare state

Finally, it is important to secure widespread public support for the welfare state. That means ensuring that income transfers are seen to efficient and fair, being hostile to all fraud, and being supportive of those who can be helped to develop the means of supporting themselves. The welfare state should provide pathways out of poverty. It also means that state provision of goods and services should be cost effective. As Nicholas Barr has argued,

> the welfare state exists not only to help the poor. It also exists because it is efficient at providing services that the market would supply badly, if at all. The Welfare State is therefore relevant to the whole population (Barr, 1992).

The welfare state and transition economies

The following chapters analyse various aspects of the welfare state in transition economies. The objective is not to provide a specific blueprint. Instead, it is to provide a framework of analysis that can be used to determine an efficient structure for social policy within the new market economies of central and eastern Europe.

Conclusions

- In a number of important respects (inequality, poverty, participation, unemployment) the transition has led to a sharp decline in welfare. This decline varies between countries. Russia and Ukraine appear to have been the most badly affected. Other countries, such as Romania, Bulgaria, and Lithuania have also experienced significant welfare declines.
- Welfare policy in the transition countries has evolved substantially since the beginning of the transition. Some benefits

for which the need has increased the most (eg unemployment benefits) have often become the most inadequate. A major role has been played by transition-specific problems such as the need to *re*build the public sector so that it is capable of delivering efficient and high quality programmes.

- Social programmes are subject to financial, administrative and economic constraints.
- Welfare programmes normally reduce inequality and poverty. As far as their effect on efficiency is concerned, this may be positive or negative, depending on the circumstances. Welfare programmes may reduce efficiency ('welfare without work', the poverty trap) or increase it (by raising participation, improving the health and increasing the skills of the population).
- It is too simple to interpret the apparent achievements of the US in generating employment as an example of the trade-off between equity and efficiency. The apparent achievements are much less impressive when account is taken of demographic and penal factors and of disguised unemployment. The latter can trap some workers in a low wage ghetto.
- The contemporary challenge in all Europe is to design social programmes which not only have a positive effect on income distribution and poverty reduction but which also raise efficiency.
- The welfare state can increase efficiency because it provides goods and services (such as social insurance) that the market does not provide, or provides at high cost (eg pensions) or which for technical reasons (such as uncertainty, information problems, and their public goods character) the market cannot provide efficiently.
- The challenge for the transition countries is to design a welfare state which provides these goods and services subject to the severe constraints under which they operate and the potential inefficiency of the bureaucratic allocation of resources. Transfer payments and publicly provided goods and services should be regularly audited for value for money and correspondence to the preferences of the population.

Endnotes

1. Of course, those selling matches in the street may not be recorded as being in employment (though they might conceivably be listed as 'self-employed'). But the argument applies generally to all employment in which an individual is working at a level of productivity below that which they might attain if the economy were operating at a full employment level of output.
2. 'Inegalitarian educational system' can have various meanings, not all economically negative. What is meant here is an education system with a high expenditure per pupil sector access, to which depends on the income or wealth of parents (either directly, or indirectly, due to superior preparation, as may well be the case with respect to access to the best universities).
3. Vilfredo Pareto (1848-1923), an Italian, was Professor of Political Economy at the University of Lausanne.
4. Economists, however, have considered the case of 'Pareto-optimal redistribution'. If well-off individuals find that the presence of individuals in their society with income, education, nutrition, housing and health care standards below a certain minimal level, reduces their own well-being, then a 'Pareto-optimal redistribution' is possible. From this perspective some welfare state programmes may well be Pareto-efficient even though those who pay for them are financially worse off as a result.
5. Introducing the Fundamental Theorem of Welfare Economics, the author of a recent popular and influential textbook told his readers, 'You should now be hearing choirs of angels and choruses of trumpets. The "invisible hand" of the price mechanism produces equilibria that cannot be improved upon.' (Kreps, 1990, p200).
6. 'Perfect' markets are perfectly competitive and complete (including markets for future and contingent goods).
7. A good is a public good if, once produced, no one can be excluded from benefiting from its availability. Classic examples are national defence, control of infectious diseases, and justice.

2. Employment, education and growth

High levels of employment are the foundation of successful social policies. And successful social policies can make an important contribution to the maintenance of high levels of employment in competitive economies. This reciprocal relationship is very complex, and choosing the right priorities and the right balance is a fundamental policy problem facing those charged with the development of successful market economies. The social market economy is an approach to this conundrum that in some periods and in some countries has been very successful. But even where it has been successful, the new challenges of the 21st century are demanding new approaches to employment policy and to the welfare state.

Transformational recession and employment.

The transformational recession led to a sharp fall in formal sector employment throughout central and eastern Europe. Excluding the former GDR, formal sector employment fell from about 193 million in 1989 to less than 170 million in 1996, or by about 12 per cent (ECE 1997). The fall was most pronounced in central Europe, south-east Europe, and the Baltic countries, where on average it was about 16 per cent, and least pronounced in the CIS countries, where it was only about 11 per cent. A large number of countries now have serious problems of unemployment and economic and social marginalisation.

The fall in formal sector employment has had important – usually negative – consequences for the people concerned. It has frequently led to social exclusion, a decline in individual and family income, and a worsening of opportunities for the children. From the point of view of socio-economic transformation, some of the decline in employment was inevitable in the pursuit of medium-term, socially-desirable, goals. It is inefficient and undesirable to keep people employed indefinitely in heavy industry whose products are only needed because of the excess material-intensity and high stock levels characteristic of the old regime, and which can only survive financially by receiving subsidies from the state or delaying or failing altogether to pay wages and taxes. Moreover, where participation levels were high by international standards because of (looked at from the workers' point of view) low wage and/or pension levels, or (looked at from the employers' point of view) low labour productivity, some decline in participation *if accompanied by real wage and/or pension increases* was probably in accordance with the preferences of those who left the labour force. However, with wages and pensions remaining low in much of the region, and poverty a serious social problem, the failure of the new private sector to absorb a significant part of the labour released by the declining state sector is a major social problem.

What has happened to work in the informal sector, on which there are no reliable statistics, is uncertain. It seems that in general, comparing 1989 with 1995, the informal sector greatly expanded as a share of GDP, and that the informal sector was most important in the CIS countries (EBRD 1997, pp73-74). However, since the countries with the largest estimated shares of the informal sector in GDP in 1995 are countries where the GDP fell most (eg Georgia) this does not necessarily mean that total work in the informal sector rose. It also seems that in the central European countries the share of the informal sector in GDP has been declining since 1992. See Table 2.1.

Table 2.1: Estimated share of the informal sector in GDP

	1990	1991	1992	1993	1994	1995	1996
Belarus	12.0	15.4	16.6	13.2	11.0	18.9	19.3
Bulgaria	22.8	25.1	23.9	25.0	29.9	29.1	36.2
Czech Republic	6.0	6.7	12.9	16.9	16.9	17.6	11.3
Hungary	27.0	28.0	32.9	30.6	28.5	27.7	29.0
Latvia	12.0	12.8	19.0	34.3	31.0	34.2	35.3
Poland	15.7	n.a	23.5	19.7	18.5	15.2	12.6
Romania	22.3	13.7	15.7	18.0	16.4	17.4	19.1
Russia	12.0	14.7	23.5	32.8	36.7	40.3	41.6
Slovakia	6.0	7.7	15.1	17.6	16.2	14.6	5.8
Ukraine	12.0	16.3	25.6	33.6	38.0	45.7	48.9

Source: EBRD (1997) p74. These estimates are based on the controversial 'electricity' method, in which the size of the informal sector is inferred from an assumed relationship between actual electricity consumption and actual economic activity. For the CIS countries, they are higher than the estimates of the national statistical offices. For example, in the late 1990s, the Russian national statistical office estimated the informal sector (an estimate of which is included in the official GDP data) at only about one quarter (not two fifths) of total GDP. For alternative estimates of the size of the informal sector, using a modified 'electricity' method, see Lackó (1999).

The informal sector provides work and income, invaluable to those who cannot find work in the formal sector, and they have some advantages compared those who work in the formal sector, notably not paying income tax and social security contributions. Nevertheless, work in the informal sector is inferior to the formal sector in a number of key respects. Its participants neither enjoy regular pay, nor the benefits paid for by social security systems (pensions, sick pay, medical care, child benefits). They do not have paid holidays, work safety, promotion prospects, security of employment (for example, formal notice periods) nor protection against arbitrary actions by the boss.

High unemployment in transforming economies

In a number of countries that are making substantial progress with transformation, unemployment has risen to levels that are high relative to the low unemployment EU countries, although not dissimilar to the higher unemployment EU countries. But this has been accompanied by a gradual restructuring of the economy, contributing to the Europeanisation of the countries concerned. In central Europe the sectoral allocation of labour is shifting towards EU patterns, labour productivity is rising fast, exports to the EU have increased substantially, and the income and productivity gap with the EU is becoming smaller. In 1996, according to the results of the International Comparison Project, per capita GDP at purchasing power parity in Slovenia had already reached the Greek level and the Czech level was 96 per cent of the Greek level (Greece is the EU member state with the lowest per capita GDP measured in purchasing power parity). In perhaps the most successful of the transformation countries, Poland, unemployment, after reaching a high level, has fallen in response to sustained economic growth, from a peak of 17 per cent in July 1994 it had fallen to 9.5 per cent by August 1998. In eastern Europe as a whole[1], unemployment at the end of 1997 was 21 per cent below its peak of March 1994.

Low unemployment and limited transformation

In the CIS countries, unemployment, both as officially measured by the national statistical offices and as calculated or estimated according to the ILO methodology, has remained low relative to central and south-east Europe and to the decline in output.

In September 1997 registered unemployment was only 0.4 per cent in Uzbekistan, 2.4 per cent in Ukraine and 3 per cent in Belarus. Although, *ceteris paribus*, these are admirable figures, in fact other things are certainly not equal. They are only achieved by making registration as unemployed difficult or unremunerative, and by the persistence of high levels of low productivity (or even negative value added) employment. In Belarus the authorities discourage managers from laying off workers, mostly by commands to produce and to export at all costs.

Data recently published by the CIS Statistical Committee indicated that on average in the CIS countries actual unemployment was three to four times officially registered unemployment (ECE, 1998, p126). Disguised unemployment is rife in organisations that are either formally in the public sector or de facto dependent on finance from the state budget or state-owned banks. Much activity does not merit the term 'employment' because wages are not paid on time. Some does not merit the term 'work' since employees in fact do very little. In some countries, Belarus is an example, there is a 'discouraged manager effect' – the authorities discourage managers from laying off workers.

This situation is not compatible with a gradual development of an efficient social-market economy, or more generally with the Europeanisation of the socio-economic system. Indeed, it is not viable in more than the short run, as was demonstrated by the deep economic crisis in Bulgaria in 1996-97 that was the result of attempting to prop up uneconomic enterprises with bank 'loans'. The 1998 financial crisis in Belarus is another indicator of the non-viability of such a strategy.

The need to continue transformation

Despite the unemployment levels in transition countries, it is necessary to continue the transformation process. In some cases, the incomplete nature of transformation has led to situations that are unacceptable from the point of view of the social democratic conception of employment. An example is the use of intimidation and strong-arm tactics in labour relations in Russia, which is unfortunately just one aspect of the general criminalisation of the economy in that country (and is not unknown in other CIS countries). On a number of occasions in recent years, trade union activists have been physically attacked. Attempts have even been made to murder them (Gordon, 1997, p35). Basic legal protection for workers and their representatives against arbitrary violence by the bosses is a minimal element of a civilised employment policy. More generally, observance of the law on trade union recognition, employment rights and social insurance cannot, in some countries, be taken for granted. Trade unions play an essential role in civil society. Unfortunately, in some countries the transition from pseudo trade unions to real trade unions that represent their members and enjoy recognition and respect both by employers and by the wider society, is far from complete.

Furthermore, there are still serious delays in the payment of wages. Delays in wage payments, or payment in kind, whether as a result of IMF monetary targets, the survival of non-viable enterprises, the 'privatisation' of part of the income of a firm, or of the theft of intended wage payments by crooked intermediaries, are unacceptable. They are a grotesque departure from the basic operating procedures of a market economy. Owners of firms that do not pay wages on time should lose their ownership. It should be transferred automatically to the employees, who should decide whether to hire new managers, keep the existing managers, take over the management themselves, or liquidate the firm, dividing the proceeds among themselves. (Unfortunately, this approach is not applicable to the budget sector and public utilities, where the biggest problems often exist.)

Policies to combine low unemployment with transformation

If there is to be any hope of attaining low unemployment during transformation, institutional and structural change must be combined with policies that ensure high and growing levels of demand and the pursuit of appropriate supply-side policies.

The necessary institutional and structural changes were set out in *Transformation and Integration* (Eatwell *et al*, 1995).

The growth of demand is composed of the growth of exports, investment, consumption and government expenditure. Export growth depends on external markets, exchange rate policy, domestic cost levels, and the ability of domestic entrepreneurs to respond to market opportunities. Investment depends largely on expectations about the growth of profitable domestic and foreign markets, as well as the creation of an honest and competent bureaucratic framework and appropriate reform of financial institutions to ensure a steady flow of finance into real investment from both home and abroad. It also depends on the absence of (and perceived absence of) extortion, corruption and criminality. Consumption is mainly determined by incomes, present, past and expected in the future. Government expenditure is determined by government revenues and fiscal policy, and by the need to maintain an appropriate fiscal balance in the light of monetary policies and inflationary pressures.

The appropriate policies to achieve a steady growth in demand depend very much on the circumstances of the country concerned. For small countries with high shares of exports in national income, wage restraint (to generate growth of exports and investment) can be of great importance. Hence the importance of social partnership in countries such as Netherlands, Austria and Sweden. In West Germany in the 1950s, an undervalued exchange rate was also an important stimulus to demand. A tax system and tax levels that allow successful companies to retain a substantial part of their gross profits, is another important factor. Well over 90 per cent of all corporate investment in advanced industrial economies is financed from retained profits. Profits are also necessary to attract finance into more risky ventures. Stable fiscal and monetary policies are also necessary. Policymakers must provide a stable and predictable macroeconomic environment in which long-term investment decisions can be taken with some confidence.

On the supply side, policy areas that play a particularly important part in the promotion of employment are education policy, active labour market policies, and the promotion of social cohesion.

Education

Education for, and training in, the demands of a competitive market economy are key elements in the development of a successful employment strategy in the transformation countries (Laporte and Schweitzer, 1994; World Bank, 1996, Chapter 8). Numerous projects to improve and reshape education and training, some purely domestic, some bilateral, and some supported by the EU and the World Bank, have already been implemented or are under way today.

Education policy is important for two reasons. First, a widespread economic phenomenon throughout the world is the strong negative relationship between education and unemployment. This suggests that education can give people the skills to enable them to secure and keep jobs, even when the growth of demand is relatively low. Secondly, it is clearly necessary to provide people with the skills that are in demand in the labour market, so as to enable firms to recruit the people they need. Higher growth rates will stimulate firms themselves to invest in the skills of their labour force, but this process is greatly facilitated by a well-educated labour force, with the adaptability that derives from high quality in-work training[2].

A major policy issue facing the transformation countries is the financing of education. State budgets are everywhere under pressure, and even with a resumption of economic growth resources are bound to be extremely scarce. Competition for resources between the public and private sectors, and within the public sector between the rival claims of pensions, education, defence, servicing the public debt, and so on, mean that funding for education will inevitably remain under pressure. Cuts in educational expenditures have been extensive (UNICEF, 1998, p26). Perhaps the most extreme example is Bulgaria, where real state educational spending appears to have fallen by about three-quarters (sic) between 1989 and 1996. Fortunately, this is an extreme case and not representative. Romania, Poland and Slovenia seem not to have experienced cuts in state educational expenditures.

There have been declines in the pay of teachers (in particular in the FSU) and non-payment of teachers (common in Russia). So miserable did the financial and social situation of many Russian teachers become, that a recent Russian book on the economic sociology of the transformation (Kosals and Ryvkina 1998 p325) observes that 'In post-Soviet Russia teachers have been one of those professional groups whose situation suddenly became almost tragic'. Their numerous strikes have had little effect. The willingness of most Russian teachers (who are mainly women) to carry on working conscientiously for a pittance has been a remarkable tribute to their dedication to their pupils and their profession (although in many cases it results from the lack of alternatives of immobile second earners in an economy in deep decline). The poor pay of Russian teachers (especially outside Moscow), and their frequent need to take on additional work, is most unlikely to have improved the quality of their teaching.

In addition there has been neglect of the maintenance of school buildings (common throughout the region), and the introduction of charges for higher education (for example, in Hungary). In some countries, such as Bulgaria, Moldova and FYR Macedonia, the heating of schools in winter has become a serious problem. (In FYR Macedonia the EU has funded oil to heat schools in winter.) In many countries the provision of school meals has significantly declined. This is the case in Russia, Belarus, Slovakia and Bulgaria. On the other hand, in Hungary between 1989 and 1996 the provision of school meals remained roughly constant[3]. The costs of education for children and their parents (both direct costs such as textbooks and shoes, and opportunity costs such as the cut in family income resulting from loss of work done on the family farm), migration[4], and the decline in public administration, have led to a decline in the proportion of certain age groups attending schools (see Table 2.2).

Table 2.2 Basic education enrolments
Gross enrolment rates[a], percentage of 6-7 to 14-15 age group

	1989	*1996*
Albania[b]	90.8	87.6[c]
Bulgaria	98.4	93.6
Estonia[d]	98.1	92.2
Latvia[d]	95.8	89.5
Russia[d]	93.0	91.4
Ukraine[d]	93.1	90.3

a These are the total number of children enrolled, divided by the number of children in the age group. Hence an increase in the number of children repeating the year 'improves' the statistics. Furthermore, inaccurate estimates of the number of children in the relevant age cohort will distort them. In addition, the figures are for enrolments at the beginning of the school year, not for attendance. The accuracy of the figures for Russia and Ukraine, especially for 1989, is uncertain. UNICEF (1995, p147 and 1997, p159) gives quite different figures for Russian secondary enrolments.

b 6-13 years.

c 1994.

d 7-15 years.

Source: UNICEF (1998) pp20-21 and 111.

The situation shown in Table 2.2 – if the data is accurate – is alarming. In some countries the proportion of children receiving education has fallen significantly during the transformation period. Currently, in a number of countries, about one in ten children are being deprived of schooling.

Inequality has, in many cases, increased both in provision and educational achievement. For example, in Hungary there has been an in increase in the disparity in learning achievements between children in the main cities and in the villages (UNICEF, 1998, pp45-46). Another important development has been the growth of private education, see Table 2.3. Where private schools are fully privately financed, even though they may be a source of social inequality, their existence at least reduces the fiscal burden of education. But in central Europe private secondary schools are heavily subsidised by the state.

Table 2.3 Secondary school pupils in private schools in 1996-97

Czech Republic	7%
Hungary	8%
Poland[a]	4%
Slovakia	12%

a 1995-96

Source: UNICEF (1998) p83

In Russia too, educational inequalities seem to have increased. According to a recent study: 'Under the banner of 'increased choice', all these concerns point paradoxically to diminished educational opportunities for many children, especially those who are rural, less affluent, or less well-connected – regardless of their individual merit... As Russian society becomes increasingly stratified in terms of wealth, Russian education is increasingly stratified in terms of opportunity' (OECD 1998, pp79 and 82).

Another example of educational inequality, concerns ethnic minorities. One such case is the situation of Roma children. A 1992 study showed that in Romania only 51 per cent of Roma children of ten years of age regularly attended school. 14 per cent had stopped school, 16 per cent went to school occasionally, and 19 per cent had never been to school (UNDP 1999, p57).

In the complex and difficult situation throughout the transition economies it is important to stress a number of basic facts.

First, a well-educated and well-trained labour force plays a key role both in economic development and in saving on welfare expenditures. As Laporte and Schweitzer (1994, p260) have observed:

> At least since the development of human capital theory in the 1960s...economists have realised that high level of education and training are crucial determinants of a country's economic success. This has been confirmed most recently by two studies (World Bank 1991, 1993). The latter examined the determinants of success of the East Asian 'tigers' and identified their high levels of education, from basic education to research, as one of the key factors distinguishing them from their peers. But quite apart from economic competitiveness, there is another reason to emphasise education and training now. Failure to invest in the education of young people will generate large downstream costs for the state and the individual because the poorly educated make up a large proportion of persons who are unemployed and living in poverty, and they consume a disproportionate share of public services and public expenditures.

Second, the provision of a good quality primary and secondary education for all is a basic public responsibility. It has high returns both to individuals and society as a whole, and the recipients often have little or no current incomes with which to purchase education for themselves. Moreover, the recipients, particularly children and often their parents too, seldom have either the information, or the ability to act on the information, which would enable them to make efficient educational choices.

Third, since in many countries there are substantial regional income inequalities, decentralization of educational services and a greater role for the market (if any) should be combined with national policies to ensure minimum standards and reasonable equity throughout the country. This is important to ensure equality of opportunity and social integration.

Fourth, the role of private funding is bound to be small. Private provision is inefficient (serving only a part, usually a small part, of the whole community), makes equality of opportunity impossible, and does not take account of the wider impact of education in its contribution to the economic growth of the whole country. Nevertheless there are some areas, particularly in tertiary education, where information is readily available and understood. In these circumstance contributions by the users or their parents may be necessary as in partial fee payments by university students where a loan system operates. Furthermore, in some areas such as vocational courses for adults (driving schools, language schools, word processing courses) where the courses are short, the individual benefits large, and the recipients have an income, wealth or access to credit, private provision and user payment are entirely sensible.

Fifth, education tends to suffer because of the inefficiency of the budgetary process. Instead of 'plan bargaining' or refusal by the Ministry of Finance to meet budgetary commitments, objective criteria and transparent processes for allocating resources, should be introduced. Of course, major political disagreements over the balance of government spending would remain. But at least they would be conducted within a better framework of economic information.

Sixth, the content of education requires continual modernisation in the light of the need to develop the talents of all pupils, the need for everyone to be able to participate in the new societies that are being created, the changing requirements of the labour market, the changing wishes of the participants in the educational process, and changing technology. Particularly important is the need to respond to the strengths and weaknesses of the inherited system. For example, international science and maths tests on nine and thirteen year olds in 1991, showed that Hungary, Slovenia and the Soviet Union scored very well on awareness of facts and on application of facts, but much less well on the use of knowledge in unanticipated circumstances (World Bank 1996 p125). The Third International Maths and Science Study (TIMSS), held in 1994-95, showed that by international standards the level of maths and science knowledge of 13-14 year olds in central and eastern Europe was good. Children in the Czech Republic, Slovakia, Slovenia, Bulgaria, Hungary and Russia achieved mean scores in maths and science that were above the OECD average and ahead of children in the UK, Germany and the US. On the other hand, the 1994 International Adult Literacy Study (IALS), which considered adults rather than children, and focussed on 'functional literacy' which gauges the ability to perform tasks encountered in everyday life, including at the workplace, showed that adults in Poland (the only transition country included) scored on average well below the 12 Western countries covered by the study. Poland also had an unusually wide range of scores in functional literacy (Micklewright 1999). This suggests that many

Polish adults are poorly prepared to compete in an enlarged EU and points to the need for adult education and (re)training.

Seventh, there is a difficult trade-off between the number and salaries of teachers. Since the resources available for education are limited, it will often be the case that paying teachers decent salaries is only possible by reducing their numbers. Such a policy may encounter strong resistance, as was shown by the strikes in Poland in 1993 when measures were announced to increase salaries whilst reducing staff numbers by one third and increasing hours of work.

Finally, a difficult issue facing education policy-makers is the language of instruction in multinational states (an analogous issue is the role of denominational schools). The use of minority languages helps to preserve the language and identity of the national group concerned, but there is danger that it will strengthen divisions in society; similarly, with denominational schools. Ideally, an important function of education is to develop social capital, but divided educational systems, as in Northern Ireland (divided by religion) and Estonia (divided by language) are a factor contributing to the maintenance of social tension. Fortunately, there are already many educational programmes in the transformation countries to promote democratic values (UNICEF 1998, pp59-61). These are very constructive, and merit external funding where necessary (which already exists in some cases).

Active labour market policies

Some attempts to alleviate the burdens of unemployment have made matters worse. High unemployment benefits can lengthen unemployment periods (and increase the aggregate unemployment rate) by enabling the unemployed to be more choosy about which jobs they accept. High social payments that are deemed the responsibility of the individual entrepreneur can result in a level of gross labour costs to employers that significantly reduces the incentive to increase employment, especially of unskilled workers. Means-tested welfare benefits which result in a high marginal (effective) tax rate on those who take up jobs can make employment financially unattractive. This is the 'poverty trap'.

It is widely accepted that these policies, whilst they provide an income for the unemployed, limit the possibility of their moving into work. Hence a very wide spectrum of political opinion in the West is now sceptical of widespread 'welfare without work' and supports measures to link welfare benefits to the creation of employment opportunities, particularly among the unskilled and those with a weak position in the labour market. There is a mutual responsibility between the state and the unemployed. It is the responsibility of the state to provide opportunities for the unemployed to obtain work and the means of securing work (such as skills). It is the responsibility of individuals to take up the opportunities on offer.

Active labour market policies, traditionally associated with the Nordic countries, aim to keep unemployment low by running an effective employment service, providing training, and directly creating jobs by means of employment subsidies, public sector employment, and public works programmes. In the US and UK, policy in the 1990s has attempted to stimulate employment by reducing welfare benefits and increasing the net income of low paid workers. The transformation countries can learn from these experiences. There is a danger of the allocation of substantial resources to badly-designed welfare expenditures that create a stratum of the population that is excluded from the labour market. They can also learn the merits of active labour market policies, particularly when combined with a social security system that ensures that it is worthwhile to work. This mix of policies is efficient from a fiscal point of view and contributes to social integration. A transformation-specific reason for the use of active labour market policies is the relatively low outflow from unemployment in those countries, so that unemployment there can be characterised as a stagnant pool (Boeri 1994).

There is already considerable experience in the transformation countries with the use of active labour market policies. An example is the programme 'Molodezhnaya praktika' introduced in Moscow in 1995 (Rimashevskaya and Yakovleva 1998, p106). This provides temporary work experience for young people between 16 and 26, who have completed their education and have been registered as unemployed for more that three months. In Poland the three most important active labour market policies are training and retraining, wage subsidies, and public works (ie the direct provision of employment by the state). However, compared with western OECD countries with similar unemployment levels, Poland spends little on active labour market policies and most of its labour market expenditures are for traditional passive programmes, ie unemployment benefit. Terrell and Sorm (1999) have shown that in the Czech republic in 1992-94 counselling services for the unemployed, administered by the local labour offices, lowered the unemployment duration of groups that tended to have the longest spells of unemployment spells: women, Roma, the handicapped, the less educated, and those who had been unemployed before. This study also found that the right to unemployment benefit did lead to a lengthening of spells of unemployment, but that this effect was relatively small compared to those found in the US. Terrell and Sorm (1999 pp59-60) concluded that the Czech combination of passive and active labour market policies was 'effective in improving the functioning of the labour market in the transition period. Overall, from the political economy standpoint, our results suggest that by providing support to job seekers and assisting them in finding employment, the UCS [unemployment benefit] and ALMPs [active labour market policies] increased the social acceptability of the painful economic transition'.

The evaluation of active labour market policies in Poland by Kluve *et al* (1999) and in Slovakia by Lubyova and van Ours (1999) enable two important conclusions to be drawn about the effects of the programmes, as implemented in those two countries. First, participation in training or retraining schemes, ceteris paribus, increases the chance of an unemployed person finding a new job. This was also a finding of the study by O'Leary *et al.* (1998) that evaluated active labour market policies in Poland and Hungary. Secondly, some active labour market programmes have negative effects. This means that the participants would have had a greater chance of securing a job without them. Partly this may be a 'stigmatisation' effect, ie in the eyes of potential employers participants in such programmes are low productivity workers. More important, certainly in Poland, seems to be a 'churning' effect, where long-term unemployed are put in such programmes to enable them to requalify for the payment of unemployment benefits. Some negative effects on the chances of re-employment were also found in Poland and Hungary.

The evaluation of the Slovenian public works programme in 1992-96 by Vodopivec (1999) concluded that it increased the chances of participants finding a job immediately after leaving the programme, but reduced them in the longer term. This longer-term negative effect could be related to stigmatisation. The positive effects on employability were found to be particularly large for younger workers. The study also found that participation in the Slovenian public works programme reduced the proportion of the unemployed who left the labour force altogether. An interesting feature of the Slovenian public works programme is that unlike the classical public works programme focussing on the utilisation of unskilled labour (traditionally, for example, road building), it focuses mainly on social services and education, ie on white collar, more education-intensive activities. In this respect it follows the German ABM programme (*Arbeitsbeschaffungsmassnahmen*) that has been used in the five new Länder of the German Federal Republic.

Several studies have suggested that active labour market policies have disproportionately benefited men. For example, officials have used them to prolong the period of unemployment benefits of male heads of households.

In general, experience shows that to be successful active labour market policies require substantial funding *and* institutional capacity. The mixed results on the effectiveness of active labour market programmes thrown up by recent research suggests the need to carefully monitor such programmes, continuing or intensifying those that work well, and amending or cancelling those that are ineffective. It should be noted, however, that even if active labour market policies do not lead to all their participants immediately obtaining stable jobs or becoming self-employed, they at least interrupt what might otherwise have been a continuous spell of unemployment. This in itself may be positive from the standpoint of income, self-esteem, maintenance or enhancement of human capital, and continued participation in the labour market.

Social integration

Social exclusion is a phenomenon of major importance throughout Europe, west and east. Everywhere there is a danger that 'identity politics' (the tendency of people to identify with one ethnic group or another) or the working of the labour market or the working of the welfare state, will exclude a significant group of the population from normal society. In extreme cases this may generate a hereditary underclass, such as the Roma[5]. That is both socially undesirable and detrimental for economic growth. International experience shows, as the World Bank frequently emphasises, that inequality can have an adverse effect on growth. Ways to tackle this danger include: the universal provision of good quality pre-school, primary and secondary education, development of active labour market policies, adoption and implementation of anti-discrimination legislation, and the devotion of additional resources to the education of the affected minorities. It is job creation through economic growth that is a fundamental mechanism of social integration.

The importance of growth

Economic growth depends on a wide variety of demographic, geographic, political, institutional and economic factors. As far as the transformation countries are concerned, important factors are: ending the drain on the country's resources from uneconomic activities inherited from the old regime (for example, uneconomic coal mines), reducing the cost of expensive transfer programmes (such as pensions in Poland, the cost of which was substantially raised by the 1989-90 policy of 'shock therapy'[6]), stimulating the new private sector, and enforcing private contracts and property rights. The inability of the state to protect entrepreneurs from the demand to pay a substantial part of their turnover to protection racketeers, together with the need to pay substantial bribes to officials and politicians, combined with frequent inspections and substantial tax payments, are serious constraints on economic growth in the CIS countries.

Another important goal should be macroeconomic stability. This requires both fiscal discipline and timely attention to macroeconomic disequilibria (as in Hungary in 1995). Pursuing unsustainable policies till the last moment, and then suddenly abandoning them in favour of radically different policies, as in Russia in August 1998, is simply a recipe for a prolonged unsatisfactory performance.

Real jobs

It is possible to keep ILO-defined unemployment low not only by providing well-paid jobs in the formal sector, but also by enabling part of the population to scrape a living in low income sectors such as agriculture (as in Romania) or in low-paid services (as in the US) or in the irregularly paid sector (as in Russia). Indeed, throughout central and eastern Europe, a high proportion of current employment fails to generate adequate incomes. This is clearly shown by the need for many people to have several jobs because they are unable to earn a basic living from just one, and by poverty among those who do have a job.

Such states of affairs can, under some circumstances, be better than nothing, But they are entirely unsatisfactory in the medium run. The objective of social democrats is high participation rates in high productivity occupations that provide good incomes and favourable employment conditions. The aim is 'real jobs'. To provide the right sort and scale of employment requires an internationally competitive business sector and a public sector, which are large and efficient. It also requires a labour force that is well enough educated to fill the vacancies in modern high productivity industries. The key policy variables in attaining these goals are domestic investment, foreign direct investment, education and innovation.

In the short run there is often a trade-off between the creation of jobs and conditions of employment. By reducing employment costs to the employer and social benefits to (former) employees, it may in the short run be possible to generate more employment. In the medium run there are some offsetting effects since growing employment costs stimulate technical progress (by forcing firms to invest in labour saving machinery), provide a market for new products, and facilitate the 'creative destruction' of inefficient, slowly innovating, businesses (Kleinknecht, 1998). The road to the medium run creation of real jobs is not the worsening of employment conditions, but the pursuit of policies that provide the framework within which high productivity firms and public sector organisations can flourish.

The transformation countries have to develop competitive industries and services within an international environment marked both by regional integration and by globalisation. Regional integration, such as the EU and CEFTA, expands the possibilities of the division of labour. Specialisation increases and trade grows. In the EU regional integration has been a great success. For the EU 12, between 1960 and 1995, intra-EU trade in goods more than doubled as a proportion of their GDP (*European Economy*, 1996). At the same time, regional integration limits the freedom of action of the member states and creates the need for region-wide instruments to manage the economies concerned effectively. Perhaps the main economic gain the transformation countries that join the EU can hope to achieve is an investment boom resulting from perceived profit opportunities and leading to a thorough modernisation of their economies. Joining requires that the countries concerned meet EU standards, including state regulation of the market, measures to ensure competition, and the opening up of state purchases to EU-wide competition. It also requires a business sector that can face up to competition from wealthy and efficient EU firms (see Eatwell *et al* 1997). CEFTA started badly and now needs both widening and deepening. Substantial progress in widening was made on 1 January 1999 with the accession to CEFTA of Bulgaria, Romania and Slovenia.

The novelty and importance of globalisation are often exaggerated: the intercontinental transmission of technology and disease goes back centuries, comparisons are often distorted by using the dirigiste post-World War II years as a basis rather than the liberal 1913, and as far as the visible trade of EU members is concerned, globalisation is less important than regional integration. Nonetheless, it is clear that today a country's fate can be greatly influenced by events on the other side of the world. A considerable advantage in dealing with these storms is derived from the sheer scale and integration of the European Union.

Conclusion

The best social policy is full employment. However, the kind of full employment which existed under the old regime and which exists in Ukraine today, is incompatible with the goals of the transformation process. The challenge to policy-makers is to recognise their responsibility to devise policies that generate 'real jobs' on a sufficient scale to combine low unemployment with transformation. This necessitates continuation of the transformation process and implementation of job creation both on the demand and on the supply sides. On the supply side, education and training, active labour market policies (such as counselling, (re)training and public works), and attention to social cohesion, are particularly important. On the demand side, the attainment and continuation of economic growth is of fundamental importance for job creation and for economic modernisation. Both aspects of employment policy must today be formulated and implemented in an environment characterised both by regional and global integration.

Endnotes

1. 'Eastern Europe' in this context means Albania, Bosnia & Herzogovina, Bulgaria, Croatia, Czech Republic, Hungary, Poland, Romania, Slovakia, Slovenia, FYR Macedonia, and Yugoslavia.
2. It is sometimes suggested that although there is a positive individual return to education there is no social return since education simply leads to a redistribution of unemployment. This can undoubtedly sometimes be the case. However, this point should not be overstated. Education or training may genuinely make a person more productive; and empirical studies suggest that the uneducated are fired quicker because the costs to the employer of firing them are lower than those of educated workers (Ours and Ridder 1995). Finding and integrating valuable higher educated workers into a firm's labour force costs employers money. Hence they are reluctant to let such workers go. As a result, schooling may reduce the cyclical variation in employment and thereby the average unemployment rate. Accordingly, there is normally a positive social return to investment in education
3. Under the conditions that currently exist in some CIS countries and Bulgaria, the provision of free school meals may have a non-nutritional benefit, having a positive effect on school enrolment and attendance.
4. In Russia the population registration system can prevent the children of mobile workers receiving education. For example, people who move to Moscow without official registration there, may find their children are excluded from Moscow schools.
5. The number of Roma in Bulgaria, the Czech Republic, Hungary, Romania, and Slovakia seems to be between three and five million (see *Transitions*, September 1997, pp22-23). It seems that, far from assisting their social integration, transition, with its stress on the bottom line and highly educated labour, has increased their social marginalisation. Unfortunately, intolerance towards the Roma is widespread. They are frequently victims of mob or police violence. See also the Introduction and chapter 6.
6. The burden of Polish pensions was reduced by indexing them to real wages at a time when wages were falling. This became an intolerable burden when real wages rose rapidly.

3. Health

The triple reform challenge

The transition economies inherited a daunting set of health policy challenges and a decade later the overall progress report is clearly unsatisfactory. As broad generalisations: the health of the population in central and eastern Europe has only slightly improved and has deteriorated relative to that of the EU (see Table 3.1), satisfaction with health services remains low, and 'informal' payments to health personnel (bribes that are destructive of basic medical ethics and morale) remain the pervasive norm, estimated as starting at 30 per cent of official salaries (Saltman and Figueras 1997, pp35, 95; Balabanova 1995; von Bredow 1995, Preker and Herbert 1995).

Table 3.1 Life expectancy at birth: the health gap

	1989	*1992*	*1994*	*1996*
EU countries	76.34	77.00	77.40	77.59
East-Central Europe	70.96	70.90	71.24	71.63
Baltic and CIS	69.57	68.48	65.85	66.81

Source: World Health Organisation, Health for All Database (http://www.who.dk)

There is, of course, far more to health than simple survival, and mortality statistics capture only part of the gap. They are used here, rather than indicators of illness (morbidity measures) for the simple reason that they provide good international comparisons and comparisons over time. This is not so for morbidity.

Although the relationship between mortality and morbidity is never simple, there is a great deal of evidence which suggests that both objective measures of illness and subjective perceptions have followed the pattern painted by the cruder measure, mortality. A report of the WHO Regional Office for Europe (1998) on the overall situation in Europe indicates this in a variety of ways. An important example is the fact that tuberculosis cases have soared in the CIS and risen gradually in a number of countries of east-central Europe. The loss (and then recovery) of public health capacity in vaccination in the CIS was reflected in the early 1990s by the return of diphtheria to those countries. This region had more than 90 per cent of the diphtheria cases reported worldwide between 1990 and 1995, with 4000 dying out of a reported 150,000 cases. Survey data reveal that the health gap is even perceived this way, with some exceptions, by the people themselves, as expressed in the reduced proportion of a given age group who assess their health as being 'good' or 'very good'.

The use of mortality as a vivid and reliable indicator can, however, be misleading in some instances. The most clear-cut example is in the evaluation of women's health. Women's coping strategies, resilience and lifestyle differences appear to have insulated them to a certain degree from the mortality crisis in some of the severely effected countries of the region. This has led to an underemphasis on reform of health care for women, and in particular on the need for improvements in reproductive health.

Even so, mortality statistics reveal that women's apparent advantage in transition countries disappears with age. Life expectancy differences between men and women are distinctly wider in the east at age 0. But by age 65 there is no clear east-west divide in the number of additional years men and women can each expect to live, having reached that point.

If life expectancy and overall health have been slow to improve in central and eastern Europe, one overall change which offers some long-term hope is that there has been a significant increase in the proportion of GDP going to health care. Most countries of the region have introduced forms of 'social insurance', normally termed the Bismarck model, and those that have not, plan to do so as soon as it may be feasible. There is no evidence in western Europe to suggest that social insurance is superior to tax-based systems in utilising given resources. But the extra 2 to 2.5 per cent of GDP obtained in those transition countries which have made the switch did not crowd out public expenditure and did produce some improvement in health funding (Saltman and Figueras 1997, p34). Nonetheless, in the absence of clear gains in the effectiveness of health care, the main impact seems to have been to increase the tax and social insurance 'wedge' between labour costs to employers and take-home pay. This is admitted even by those who have been partisans of a radical shift towards market mechanisms in health care (Orosz, Ellena and Jakab 1998).

The situation in the countries of the former Soviet Union is far worse. There was a dramatic decline in life expectancy, which reached a low in

1994 and subsequently recovered only partially (Table 3.1). (The Baltic states shared these mortality figures, but may otherwise more appropriately be considered with the bulk of the countries of east-central Europe.) The generally much greater falls in output and GDP in the FSU placed a far greater strain on the health care systems. Even worse, the general and enthusiastic transition in CIS countries to 'compulsory medical insurance funds' has proved, in most cases, to be a transition to chaos in finance, organisation and responsibility for health care. The most egregious evidence of this was the initial announcement in August 1998 that the reserves of the Russian regional insurance funds had been, by government order, held in GKOs (the now-frozen Treasury bills).

It is not the design of changes in the CIS countries that have distinguished them from east-central Europe, but the inappropriateness of attempting the most sophisticated institutional reform under what turned out to be very adverse conditions. If there is one lesson to be drawn from this grim situation, it is that *where states are weak, laissez-faire policies will fare worse, not better*. The opposite was frequently argued by many Russian reformers of the first and second waves. They failed to realise that 'governments have to be more competent to supervise contracting and other market-style arrangements than to run services directly' (Kettle 1993).

Indeed, in the European CIS it is remarkable not how badly, but how well health services have coped, in conditions which have gone from near-hyperinflation to near-demonetisation with a retreat to barter, with pervasive wage arrears (to which medical workers have been amongst the front line of victims), budgets subject to frequent and arbitrary sequestration, and rampant corruption (which has included, *inter alia*, senior medical officials profiting from pharmaceutical imports). It is pointless to consider general health reforms in countries in such acute crisis. When doctors are not paid for six months, there seems little point in discussing the role of alternative incentive structures, or the merits of continuing to enhance a family doctor system. When insulin and oncological drugs disappear from the pharmaceutical shelves in a week, then discussion of the best methods for deciding on doctors' clinical freedom in drug prescription, or how to encourage an emphasis on generic drugs, and the merits and demerits of patient co-payment, is absurd if not insulting to the people who have to live through this chaos. What is needed under such circumstances are local, educational, and incremental efforts to combat the general feeling of helplessness.

The discussion that follows will concentrate on the situation in those countries where wages are paid, where monetary transactions are more normal than barter, and where for a number of years there has been a return to economic growth. Despite these more favourable conditions, there is still a sense that something quite different should be happening in health care.

There are three basic reasons for the disappointing outcomes to date, even in this more successful part of transition Europe:

- The health status of the populations of these countries had been deteriorating for some time. This applies in particular to adult males. For the two decades before 1989 the health gap between east and west Europe had been widening (Meslé 1996). This gap is most vividly seen in the difference in life expectancy, but many other indicators of disability and illness would show the same pattern, if less dramatically. The reasons for the gap, which lie as much outside as inside the medical care systems, are considered below.

- The central and eastern European countries inherited a hierarchical health care delivery system. All health care systems today face the challenge of orienting to patients who demand more of medical care systems. All health care systems have been overly oriented to curative or palliative care, not to prevention. Most systems in the world (the Japanese is a notable exception) are still too oriented to hospitals, specialists, and treatment of individual parts of the anatomy. Nonetheless, in the two decades after 1970, there was discernible progress on these matters elsewhere in Europe, while the countries of the eastern bloc regressed. Despite the long-standing rhetoric of socialist medicine, the reality of the later period was that health promotion and prevention activities were far more developed in western Europe. There, quality primary health care received more attention, and the general education of the population (and medical professionals) included a growing understanding of the sources of good health in lifestyles, personal and social.

- In transition economies, as elsewhere, health care reform has proved to be far more complex and difficult than might have been thought. Every country in Europe today is attempting to

> reform its health care system. Across the continent a variety of policies has been tried, and a still greater variety proposed, but the empirical evidence on what works is painfully thin (Saltman and Figueras 1997, p2).

So what common trends are driving this general dissatisfaction, and why is health care reform everywhere proving so difficult? A very brief answer to this important question has three elements.

First, unequal access to health care presents ethical dilemmas not found in any other area of human consumption. Widely shared egalitarian values about access to health care, now very deeply embedded in modern society, then collide with a second basic fact.

This second basic consideration is that there is virtually no limit to the sums that might be spent on improving the quality of life and extending disability-free years. This latter fact does not mean that all medical interventions nowadays are cost-effective, or even effective. Far from it. The present 'conventional wisdom' is that perhaps 30 per cent of clinical intervention in western Europe is, at best, worthless. The problem is that we do not know which 30 per cent.

The third part of the health care reform dilemma is that far too little is known about what works, how much it costs, and what incentive structures will cause medical professionals, payers, providers and patients to respond in directions which enhance social and individual welfare. It is possible that a century from now some of today's medical practice and organisation will be regarded in the way we regard the widespread use of leeches and 19th century mental asylums. The worst part of this fundamental dilemma is the problem of information. Economists are becoming increasingly aware of the extent to which economic efficiency rests on accurate information, universally available. In medical care, however, tradition and instinct suggest reliance on experts. Patients want a sense of choice, but they also accept a situation where the supplier, especially the medical professional, tells them what they need. This is a fundamental barrier to the reform process. Attempts in Britain to circumvent this basic problem of 'supplier decision' by establishing a new 'managerial class' of medical managers seem to have created even worse problems, more perverse 'stakeholding', and even more costs. (The British model seems precisely to have been the model chosen for the 1999 Polish health care reform, now admitted by many to have ended in failure. It is not surprising that the Polish Supreme Audit Chamber or NIK found that there were 'irregularities' in reaching managerial contracts 'on extremely favourable conditions' by no fewer than 259 health care unit directors, while nurses had to strike to try to raise their average pay above the equivalent of $100 a month.)

This is the triple reform challenge. These three fundamental problems in the health care process are a basic reason why many economists, often passionate proponents of free markets in most areas of life, believe that market competition is inappropriate for the production and allocation of health care. This means that there are particular problems in reforming the health care systems of the transition economies. Nonetheless, there is evident and immediate scope for clear benefits, which can be much appreciated by the bulk of the population. Assessing how policy needs to develop requires first an understanding of the particular and genuinely unusual problems of the health of the population of this region.

The east-west health gap

One simple fact about health in the transition has gripped the popular imagination, east and west. In just three years, between 1991 and 1994, Russian male life expectancy at birth fell by six years, reaching 57.6 years at its lowest point. It is less well known that similar falls, albeit slightly less dramatic, affected women as well, and that the mortality crisis is also observable in the Baltic states, the European CIS and Kazakhstan. Millions of lives have been lost (see Ellman 1994, 1997; Shapiro 1994, 1995, 1997).

This tragic development has tended to crowd out much of the other information that is needed in order to design of effective policies. Unfortunately, for the past ten years health care reform in central and eastern Europe has been discussed in a knowledge vacuum, without prior understanding of concrete health problems, and with exclusive attention to financial and economic questions. This seems to derive both from the fiscal crisis and from a failure to understand the unique characteristics of health care as outlined in the 'triple reform challenge'.

As Table 3.1 shows, the decline in life expectancy was not universal. In the more westerly states (the Czech and Slovak Republics, Poland, Hungary, Slovenia) there were gains.

It is striking that other dimensions of transition success coincide with success on this front, even in the presence of substantial unemployment. This makes it difficult to discriminate between all the proposed causes of the mortality crisis. Weak states had weak transitions, with poor management of the health care system, declining funds for health care and a failure to reallocate resources to create a modern system. But even in stronger transition economies there remains a significant mortality gap with the West. Almost six years separates the life chances of a newborn child in east-central Europe from a child born in the EU. The Baltic and CIS states are now ten years behind. For boys in those countries, even after the acute crisis was over, the gap was still twelve years. What needs to be done? In fact, the characteristics of the Russian mortality crisis contain vital clues to an understanding of what can be done about the more chronic, but equally important, problem of the east-west mortality gap.

The following key factors link the acute crisis of the mid 1990s in the worst hit countries to the chronic position in the entire region:

- Just as the Russian crisis hit men much more women, so male health in eastern and central Europe lags behind female health. As a general rule, the worse the situation in a given country is, the greater the gap between men and women. Table 3.2 shows the key fault line between male life expectancy in east and west.
- One of the most disturbing features of the Russian mortality crisis (and that of neighbouring FSU states) was that it hit those in the prime, or working, ages hardest. The chronic gap between east and west is also most notable for this group. Two key causes account for the great part of the Russian mortality crisis: cardiovascular (heart and circulatory) diseases, especially at younger ages, and deaths from violent, or external causes. These are exactly the same causes that drove up death rates wherever there was a rise in mortality, notably in the Baltic republics. These are also the two causes that account for the great part of the longer-standing difference between the EU and non-FSU transition countries. See Table 3.3.
- These two key problems, violent death and cardiovascular death, might appear to have quite different roots. But there are some serious lifestyle issues, chiefly involving alcohol, which link them.

Table 3.2 Gap in male life expectancy, 1997

	Male life expectancy at birth 1997
Sweden	76.7[a]
Greece	75.8
Norway	74.9[b]
France	74.8
Netherlands	74.8[a]
UK	74.8
Denmark	73.1[a]
Finland	72.9[b]
Denmark	72.5
Portugal	71.2
Slovenia	71.2
Czech Republic	70.6
Slovakia	68.4[b]
Hungary	66.1[a]
Romania	65.3
Estonia	64.9
Latvia	63.9
Ukraine	62.4
Russian Federation	61.0
EU	74.2[a]
East-Central Europe	67.7
Baltic and CIS	62.2

a 1996

b 1995

Source: World Health Organisation, Health For All Database (http://www.who.dk)

Table 3.3 Contribution to differences between life expectancy, by cause and age group, in EU and central and eastern European transition countries (1993)

	All ages	*< 1*	*1-34*	*35-64*	*65+*
All causes	6.06	0.93	1.09	2.63	1.40
Cardiovascular	3.28	0.0	0.07	1.36	1.85
External or violent causes[a]	1.41	0.04	0.64	0.71	0.03
Respiratory	0.97	0.68	0.2	0.15	-0.05
Digestive	0.09	0.02	0.03	0.08	-0.04
Cancer	-0.05	0.0	0.05	0.25	-0.35
Infectious	0.47	0.30	0.10	0.08	-0.01
Undefined	0.12	-0.01	0.01	0.04	0.18
Other	-0.22	0.0	0.0	0.02	-0.20

a Accidents, suicides and murders

Source: World Health Organisation, Health For All database (http://www.who.dk)

In the case of excess and early mortality from accidents, suicide and murder, the problems lie much more in society than in hospitals. Table 3.4 sums up growing differences in mortality from these causes. Whilst the gap with the West remains enormous there has been a gradual turnaround since 1992 in central and eastern Europe and since 1994 in the Baltic and CIS. The scope for intervention is considerable. Examples include measures to enhance motor vehicle and general safety, alcohol control measures, child safety, electrical safety and fire prevention, and there is some scope for improved emergency services. Suicide intervention and support systems are in major need of expansion, though they cannot substitute for attention to the causes of increased suicide. Murder in central and eastern Europe, part of the crime explosion, is a major mortality factor only in the Baltic states. But it is a stress factor everywhere, diminishing welfare and health indirectly.

Reduction in death and disability (the other nine-tenths of the 'iceberg') should receive immediate, focused attention. It would not just add a year and a half to life expectancy in central and eastern Europe; it would change the health landscape. Although murders and suicides are more spectacular news, deaths from ordinary, everyday, accidents are the major factor. The role of alcohol is important in this regard (Leon *et al* 1997). Western experience with measures to reduce violent death is highly relevant to health policy, especially in the field of accident prevention. To the extent that there exists useful international comparative data on alcohol consumption, prices and control, it does indeed seem that deaths from violent causes have followed a loss of control over alcohol consumption. Though the degree to which this comes from the supply or the demand side remains contentious.

Table 3.4 Death from violent causes (accidents, suicides and murders) of those under 65 (per 100,000 persons)

	1989	*1992*	*1994*	*1996*
EU countries	38.10	36.38	34.28	32.76
East-Central Europe	61.78	70.21	66.24	62.57
Baltic and CIS	109.92	141.50	182.27	163.10

Source: World Health Organisation, Health for all database (http://www.who.dk)

For working age men in central and eastern Europe the situation is predictably worse (Table 3.5). But the gap with the EU countries is not so different from that for females. In the Baltic and CIS states an already

Table 3.5 Death from violent causes (accidents, suicides and murders) of males under 65 (per 100,000 persons)

	1989	*1992*	*1994*	*1996*
EU countries	57.72	55.28	52.30	49.77
East-Central Europe	99.53	115.44	108.85	102.37
Baltic and CIS	183.21	237.95	311.38	273.86

Source: World Health Organisation, Health for all database (http://www.who.dk)

very poor situation has become much worse.

To sum up: the intensity of deaths from violent causes at working-age is now almost twice as great in central Europe as in the EU, and almost five times greater further east. The absolute and relative mortality gaps are higher for males. This is one of the first indications that health promotion and a move to healthier life styles must be a central feature of health policy. Western data suggest that measures to reduce alcohol consumption can play an important part, as can many, small, everyday measures. However, it should be borne in mind that although these measures may be cost-effective, they might not be cost-saving (except to the extent that they reduce long-term disability).

The second of the two basic causes of the health gap is cardiovascular disease. This too, has an immense disability 'iceberg'. In the west it is the single most important cause of the long-term burden of ill health on the living population. (Major depression is normally considered to be the second). This set of diseases accounts for more than half of the difference between east and west in life expectancy, contributing more than three years to that statistic. A tragic size differential is found in younger age groups.

The absolute difference in deaths from all cardiovascular causes (heart attacks and strokes) is even wider than for violent death, especially among the working age population (see Table 3.6). As this is the leading cause of death, even small changes are important. One major reason for the difference in standardised mortality rates is the younger ages at which these deaths occur in eastern Europe.

The degree to which the causes of cardiovascular death lie inside or outside the medical care system are controversial, and the source of intense investigation. It is clear, however, that complex and expensive surgery, such as triple coronary bypasses, is not the basic answer. The roots of cardiovascular disease are found in social stress, lifestyle (tobacco and excess alcohol), long-term control of blood pressure, diet and exercise. Surgery and last minute heroic measures are the last, most expensive and (this is critical) apparently least effective line of defence.

Table 3.6 Death rate of under 65s, from all circulatory disease (per 100,000 persons)

	1989	*1992*	*1994*	*1996*
EU countries	65.48	60.04	55.93	53.71
East-Central Europe	144.80	152.79	144.29	142.49
Baltic and CIS	158.82	184.52	248.78	228.02

Source: World Health Organisation, Health for all database (http://www.who.dk)

In the past decade the situation first deteriorated and then improved in central and eastern Europe, reaching a level in 1996 marginally better than in 1989. On the other hand, whereas the pattern of initial deterioration followed by improvement can be observed in the former Soviet Union, the 1996 situation there was much worse than that of 1989 and very serious indeed. This is particularly important because the differences between the two regions were not so great at the outset. However, care should be taken when attempting to link mortality to the advocacy of a particular economic strategy. While there has been a marginal improvement in central and eastern Europe, in some countries, including Poland (with relatively little change in its health care system in the period considered) and the Czech Republic (which had a cost explosion while overshooting 'reform' in this sector) there have been significant improvements. But this has not been the case in Hungary.

Table 3.7 Death from cardiovascular disease, males under 65 (per 100,000 males)

	1989	*1992*	*1994*	*1996*
EU countries	98.60	90.05	83.44	80.11
East-Central Europe	209.66	227.64	216.12	213.28
Baltic and CIS	236.77	272.86	372.70	339.26

Source: World Health Organisation, Health for all database (http://www.who.dk)

The most disputed policy issue is the extent to which the improvement or deterioration in mortality is likely to derive from social and personal risk factors (smoking, alcohol and stress), and the extent to which changes in the medical system may be responsible.

- Infant mortality has generally not risen over the longer run in any of the transition countries. This was contrary to many expectations, and the implications are as yet not fully understood. It must be considered together with the remarkable fall in the birth rate across the whole region, also not yet fully explained. In a number of cases there appeared to be short-run rises in infant mortality. But the most important explanation of these were statistical artefacts, as countries adopted a definition of live births in line with international standards. The old Soviet definition counted as stillbirths many small infants who survived initially, but failed to live for a week.

While there is no dramatic and headline-grabbing crisis (though Bulgaria is a disturbing exception: see UNICEF ICDC, Regional Monitoring Report No 5, 1998) infant mortality is an important part of the explanation of the overall east-west mortality gap. Even so, given that infant mortality is reasonably closely correlated with international differences in per capita income, the gap between east and west is less wide than might be expected. The more prosperous transition countries have good records. Slovenia, for example, has an infant mortality rate (less than five per thousand), which compares favourably with the US figure, and is better than the EU average.

But overall there is a large gap. Indeed, although the Baltic and CIS countries improved their absolute level of infant mortality in 1989-96, their level relative to the EU deteriorated, whereas that of east-central Europe improved slightly. (Note that the significant early improvement in central and eastern Europe is largely due to the ending of the barbarous policies of the Ceaucescu regime in Romania. Also, the Baltic and CIS figures are distorted by the inclusion of Central Asia. The 1996 Russian rate of infant mortality, for example, was 17.5 per 1000, and the Ukrainian in 1996 about 14.5, and both have since fallen further).

Table 3.8 Infant mortality rate (per 1000 live births)

	1989	*1992*	*1994*	*1996*
EU countries	7.98	6.87	6.17	5.70
East-Central Europe	19.46	15.96	15.61	13.33
Baltic and CIS	22.97	24.06	22.80	21.14

Source: World Health Organisation, Health for all database (http://www.who.dk)

For central and eastern Europe, as indicated in Table 3.3, differences in infant deaths from respiratory and infectious disease are important. Such deaths are normally considered preventable. This suggests the need for considerable emphasis to be placed on social medicine, as opposed to excessive hopes for a high technology approach. For deaths among children in later years of life, accidents and violent deaths play an important role.

- Throughout this analysis of the health care situation, it has become clear that excess male mortality is a particularly acute problem in the transition countries. This should not, however, obscure the fact that there are also acute and specific problems of women's health care and reproductive health, attention to which is long overdue. These are reflected most vividly in the continuing high levels of maternal mortality in the CIS, and a less dramatic, but still excess, level of maternal mortality in some countries of east-central Europe, after an encouraging overall decline, led by a remarkable improvement in the Romanian situation, but also with definite improvements across the area (WHO, 1998).

The maternal mortality figures are only the tip of the iceberg of a whole series of interconnected problems, which have, at their root, the lag in the development of 'woman-friendly' reproductive and well-woman services. This is scarcely surprising in the context of systems that were deeply unresponsive to all users, one of the factors that encouraged illusions about privatization. After all, if medical personnel are treated like poorly paid low-level bureaucrats they have a tendency to act that way. Many medical services were traditionally more involved with certifying or denying rights to state benefits (maternity leave, sickness) than with health. A striking example of the lack of responsiveness to patients is the inherited system of clinics dealing with sexually transmitted diseases. These are often more concerned with 'protecting society' (by compulsory hospitalisation, informing employers, tracing contacts, withdrawing passports, etc) than with helping the person concerned (UNDP 1999 p51). As a result, not surprisingly, people have increasingly turned to private clinics or self-treatment. Making the state provide more client friendly clinics is an urgent task.

The most visible evidence of the failure of the modernisation of health care systems in their face towards women is that 'induced abortion remains the major method of family planning in the CCEE and NIS' (WHO, 1998). (The exception, Poland, where the right to abortion has been sharply restricted, is an example of the other side of the coin, an unreasonable restriction on women's choice.) With the introduction of a wider range of contraceptive possibilities, there has been a decline in the number of abortions, even in countries such as Russia and Romania, where more than 70 per cent of pregnancies continue to end in abortion. There is, however, across the board, a remaining clear gap in the abortion rate between east and west, mirroring all the other gaps. Although for some women there are now improved private facilities, the figures for abortion outcomes continue to indicate that these are often substantially less safe than in western Europe and unnecessarily unpleasant.

There is, however, a danger that women's reproductive health will become an issue seized by pro-natalist forces. The reality is that the abortion problem exposes the whole range of neglect of women's health issues, in a most dramatic form. Yet, for example, the death rate from cervical cancer is twice as high in the east as in the west of Europe, reflecting the failure to screen and to orient towards either education or prevention. Survey evidence has revealed that women do not attend ante-natal clinics on time, because, as might be expected, there are long queues, unfriendly and even hostile (often overworked) personnel, and, again, little emphasis on education or integration into social services.

Thus, here too, the dramatic 'headline grabbers' on abortion reveal an iceberg of ordinary neglect. The positive side to this is that small improvements - such as provision of good contraceptive information, free or very inexpensive contraceptives, and, above all, desperately needed information (for example, via better sex education in schools) can make such a difference. As the new freedoms have also brought a marked rise in sexually transmitted diseases, and now a rise in HIV/AIDS (often through drug use), an improvement in reproductive health is urgently needed. This urgency, however, should not be another excuse for a crash campaign. It is in the steady and real turn towards giving prevention, education and care of healthy individuals pride of place, that the real changes will come.

To sum up the overall health picture: there is a huge gap in the health status of eastern and western Europeans. Where the situation was worst, it has grown worse still. Men are more affected than women, working-age people most of all. No group, however, has been immune. Three priority areas for health policy, where real success could be achieved are: reducing death and injury from violent causes, especially accidents; reducing death and disability, especially at young-ages, from cardiovascular diseases; and continuing to improve infant mortality, especially reducing respiratory and infectious causes. Measures taken in this respect will also improve child health, of which infant mortality is simply an indicator. This is itself a critical investment in future adult health. Improvements in reproductive and well-woman care are also long overdue.

The pattern of excess death strongly suggests that social factors - stress, alcohol, tobacco, and overall public responsibility - play a large part in explaining the east-west gap, as well as the rise in those areas where it has occurred. The health care delivery system can play a critical role both in curative, and in preventive and health promotion areas. There is still substantial room to reduce death rates in areas like infectious disease. But it is the diseases of civilisation that loom the largest.

Policy recommendations: the health care delivery system and its limits

One of the very first symptoms of 'neo-liberal overshoot', in the first heady days of transition, was the passion to revolutionise unloved health care systems. This was spurred on by the belief that privatisation would tap hidden resources, and that increased spending on health care would be the key to answering the all too evident problems.

The health care privatisation programme has foundered on the rock of reality. The core of this reality is that markets only work effectively when they possess a number of well-specified characteristics (see Eatwell *et al.* 1995, pp76-81). An understanding of markets suggests that health care is not a commodity suited to market provision.

An instinctive west European distrust of a market-driven health care system usually derives from considerations of likely inequity and social exclusion. This distrust is well founded: some 37 million Americans have no health care insurance coverage. It is not, however, the equity implications of a market system in health which have kept other OECD countries away from the American model. It is the fact that the market system in health care is economically inefficient. The two most important types of market failure are:

- *The essential asymmetry of information.* The provider knows far more about the product than 99 per cent of consumers can reasonably learn. Is this operation, that laboratory analysis, the more expensive antibiotic, really needed? Is this coronary bypass necessary, despite the risk?

  The most that can hoped for is improving consumer awareness. Some have fancifully suggested that the medical market is about to see the rise of the wise, comparison-shopping consumer. Simple reflection suggests how limited is the average person's ability to search and weigh medical evidence, even when quite healthy and untroubled by a problematic diagnosis.

- *The considerable uncertainty an individual has about whether major medical care will be needed in future, and the large cost (relative to income) if it is.* Consequently, even in those few industrialised countries without a tax-based or universal social insurance system, the individual consumer does not, for example, select and pay the surgeon. Instead, the market is dominated by health insurance firms and 'health maintenance organisations'. This does not correspond to the basic structure of a market, with incentives for the health care consumer to act like a consumer. The need for the insurance companies to control spending results in an extraordinarily elaborate system of red tape. Transactions costs are very high. In the United States overheads run to as much as 25 per cent of premiums, and in Chile, which also has a regulated private insurance market, these costs have totalled more than 30 percent of average premium revenues (Hsaio 1995, page 176). By contrast the typical west European system's analogous costs are under 10 per cent, with the tax-funded UK National Health Service even lower.

A recent survey summed up the issue:

> It is because of these market failures that governments have intervened in most developed countries to legislate either for

> single payer tax financing or compulsory social insurance. The move towards universal population coverage helps to explain the increase in health service spending over time and the fact that the public share of total health services expenditure comprises the biggest element in the health service budget in nearly all OECD countries. (Ham 1997, p5).

Even in the United States, the public share of the health care budget is about 40 per cent, and the private health care finance market is subject to extensive state regulation to mitigate some of the distortions to which it would otherwise give rise.

This negative conclusion extends to the issue of competition between private insurers, which might have been thought to offer efficiency gains. Few western social insurance systems have found experiments with competition among private insurers to result in anything but increased costs and diminished solidarity[1]. As a major WHO report concluded:

> The choice of insurer is also controversial... It is sufficient to note here that only one country in the European Region (Israel) currently provides universal insurance that allows patients to choose among competing private companies. When the Dutch attempted to introduce multiple competing insurers, they found that it created insuperable obstacles to maintaining social solidarity. Competitive insurance has also proved to be a very expensive approach that offers few benefits in terms of additional services. (Saltman and Figueras 1997, page 37).

The increasing disenchantment with 'internal market' reforms in a number of countries adds to the weight of this analysis. Health care is not a commodity like any other, whose quality can easily be judged, which can be sent back if it does not work, even if it were known how it was supposed to work. Increased consumer response and responsibility is worthwhile. But it has limits, particularly for non-specialists. In health care markets competition has reduced efficiency and equity.

Consideration must also be given to the fundamental issue of solidarity. Orthodox economic theory states that cross-subsidisation is inefficient. Yet a fundamental *raison d'etre* of health care systems around the world is just such cross-subsidisation – between the well and the ill, between the young and the old, between the rich and the poor. Even in the heyday of private medicine in the US in the 1950s, doctors charged patients by their income level (subtly inquiring and coding), and local doctors in smaller communities regarded it as their responsibility to take some poorer cases on credit that would never be paid. This was not just price discrimination for profit maximisation. Considerations of 'equity' in health care are much more important than in other areas of consumption, for deep philosophical and humanitarian reasons.

There were many understandable illusions in transition economies about the possibilities of market reform and privatisation in health care, as well as a desire to escape what was seen as the dead hand of the state. Accordingly, the reform drive focused far too much on forms of health care finance, and not enough on what sort of medical care should be provided, and which incentive structures to encourage. The result is not disastrous, even if it is sub-optimal. There has been a general movement towards a social insurance 'Bismarck' system. As in many 'Bismarck' systems, the line between social insurance and state funding is blurred. On the one hand, there has been a continuing need to subsidise the social insurance funds from the budget, and, on the other hand, a loss of fiscal control. Poland, which did not initially take this route, was far more successful in cost control. It is to be hoped in the development of a new system Poland[2] will learn from the Czech cost explosion of 1992-1993 and the excessive British zeal for managerial expertise: 'men in grey suits' instead of better trained women and men in white coats.

The alternative, a system financed from general taxation, is usually termed a 'Beveridge' system. Ironically, the southern European Union states which had 'Bismarck' systems have been changing to 'Beveridge' systems, while central and eastern Europe seems headed the other way. If the basic advantage of a 'Beveridge' system is cost containment, then the basic advantage of a 'Bismarck' system is, under East European conditions, that it has proved easier to actually collect finance for health care. For this reason hypothecated, or earmarked, taxes for health care will help to secure the financing advantage of the 'Bismarck' system, while maintaining the control over costs of the 'Beveridge' system.

Preventive medicine and public health

In central and eastern Europe ambitions for improving health still centre almost entirely on more health care spending, and have not sufficiently widened beyond that. This is understandable. In fact, the majority of people anywhere in the world still place their hopes for better health on medical intervention, and the medical profession, no doubt sincerely, encourages them. Even though the academic conventional wisdom is that the health care system is less important that the social and economic conditions and lifestyles, there has been very little internalisation of this fact by policy-makers or commentators.

Of course, the scarcity of resources – even of basic drugs and instruments - must have dominated policy thinking. The legacy of the hunger for better medical care is that most central and eastern European countries are far too medicalised. The demand for better health has been translated into a demand for more health care. Yet western experience confirms that the most important improvements in health come with a definite change in life styles and with growing prosperity (economic growth is not just an economists' fixation, it is an essential component of a long-term health strategy). This suggests that a quite different set of questions should guide health policy:

- Consideration must be given to the evidence for programmes and policies that will work to change lifestyles. Health promotion activities everywhere have proved difficult, but possible, especially if the desire for instant success is eschewed, and if an experimental rather than dogmatic approach is used.

- Pragmatic means should be found to build a strengthened family or general practitioner system. This normally will require making this one of the traditional 'free professions,' but it is a lot more difficult to give this particular profession high status, as compared to hospital-based medicine.

- The proliferation of specialists should be limited. This is not merely expensive, but frequently outright disruptive for achieving health.

- Hospital care should be improved, noting that this frequently means limiting the need for it. Yet in a situation where social

> services and family care cannot cope, formulas for shortening hospital stays will simply be counterproductive. The integration of social services and health care, at the local and county level, provides the most equitable, humane and simultaneously efficient way to deal with the needs of patients and their families. In integrating community and social care with the medical system, many other gains, both in the quality of care and in the elimination of unnecessary expenditure, are possible. Many older people need a sympathetic ear as much as a doctor. The use of retired doctors as listeners has proved an admirable reform where it has been tried.

In the care systems of many transition countries there is a lag behind the EU in addressing the problem of improving the quality of dying. A move to more hospice and home care, and to better pain management, with more patient and family input, is even more overdue in the east than in the west. Some worries have been expressed about this policy, because it looks too attractive financially. But it is a clear fact that a high proportion of medical care goes into the last year of life, and it is not at all clear that this has a positive rate of return. Often it is dying that is prolonged, not living.

One of the hardest challenges is turning the existing medical care delivery systems, in short, into true public health systems. In moving to a more locally oriented and integrated system, policy makers can begin to address the problem of instilling the morale of a true service sector, which allows for consumer and community input. At this level of budgeting too, medical professionals will be more interested in the difficult question of judging what works best.

A new agenda

The key task lies in the creation of institutions and groups genuinely interested in public health. One important possibility is sponsorship of groups with some independence from the government, charged with the development and communication of a wide range of measures for health promotion.

Who will lead such a movement? The difficulty is that the best-organised actors inside the health care sector honestly do not see the problem in the same way. They know of the medicines they do not have, the tests they cannot do, and the run-down state of their equipment. Doctors have traditionally been unaware of the picture outside their windows. This holds *a fortiori* for chronically ill-paid medical staff in central and eastern Europe.

Leadership must come from political and social organisations. Yet it is not the ideal role for a political party. Indeed, a lecturing posture by political authorities is a sure-fire formula for failure in health promotion. The best position is an enabling one. This may include funding, where possible, but a certain arms-length role in delivering the message. This approach will help secure support for more administrative measures, such as increases in taxes on cigarettes and alcohol, limits on their advertising, and better state control of sales (see Crooks 1989). It is important to develop support if the policy is to be effective. The attractive aspect of effective alcohol and cigarette taxes is that these will be public health measures that are revenue-raising. Taxation, however, is just a beginning. The energetic encouragement of institutions for public health is far more important in the long run. They complement administrative measures and win support for them. Much is known today about what does and does not work in the field of health promotion. The great advantage in central and eastern Europe is that little of this knowledge has been applied there and early spectacular successes are possible.

Higher levels of spending on health care can be justified, but higher spending alone is not the key. It is critical to choose a path that gives the maximum improvement in health for the additional spending. This is not going to be in the extension of the present system, which does not use resources in the best way.

Conclusions

Overall, some very clear and basic conclusions can be drawn from the above analysis.

There is a great need for fewer, better-trained doctors in hospitals and more in primary care, and the mass introduction of modern nursing, applying best, international practice. Thriving general practice will almost certainly be a prerequisite. Elementary public health measures have been neglected, and are the most cost effective. These measures are the easiest. The rest will obviously not come overnight. It will take organisation that goes beyond the strictly professional groupings.

Serious consideration must be given to a carefully cost-contained plan to raise medical salaries, especially for the family or general doctors. There is no magic formula, but the Japanese system, with its centrality of the general practitioner, has produced the most spectacular health results in a short period of time, with remarkable cost containment. However, as Marmor (1994) notes, the Japanese do not love their successful system. It does not give them enough time and attention, and is too equitable for many middle-class tastes. Moreover, once again, in assigning credit lifestyle cannot be separated from health care.

It is not going to be easy to develop graduate nursing. Whole new curricula need to be developed. Perhaps a new language needs to be found for this profession. It needs professional status, dignity, and decent pay. It can provide the dedicated personnel who will transform the hospitals in ways neurosurgeons and information technology specialists cannot. The enhanced role for health visitors should also include policies to attract graduate-level personnel. Medical social work must be another developing profession, critical if the true integration of hospital, community and general practice is to emerge.

The special needs of children, and of integrated paediatric and community care, needs emphasis. Here too, prestige, morale and quality follow funding. Many more basic things, such as good school meals, and the famous milk, orange juice and cod liver oil of post-war Britain, may not make splendid slogans, but they will be long remembered, as will their life-long positive inheritance.

Creating a national system for health touches on all the deepest values of a society. Everyone is a stakeholder. But unless there is the widest, freest, consultation, the insiders will dominate, reform will be blocked, and the population will simply be fearful or indifferent. Consider just one simple question. Should the general practitioner be the 'gatekeeper' through whom you have to pass to be admitted to more specialist treatment? This works well in Britain, and is normal in many countries, but not in others. It seems both to improve health care, health status and cost-effectiveness. But the 'customers' need to feel secure in such a system too. Any change must, therefore, involve serious and lengthy dialogue.

Health care reform is a difficult task everywhere in the world. If this were not trouble enough, the transition economies inherited serious health problems: the sharpest indications of this have been in the vast health gap that divides the European continent. Death and disability from violent causes (often just humdrum accidents) and death from cardiovascular disease at tragically young ages are the key factors. These differences as compared with western Europe find their wellsprings as much outside the medical care delivery system as inside. Indeed, a good health care policy would not even make such sharp distinctions. As a third complicating challenge, the transition economies inherited deeply under-funded, distorted and unresponsive health care systems, characterised by low morale, low-level corruption, and bureaucracy.

In the countries of the CIS the overall economic and political climate has simply not allowed any global health reform to succeed, and a much more basic approach to crisis intervention is needed at present. The recommendations in this chapter have focused on central and eastern Europe, including the Baltics, where progress has been unsatisfactory, but where there has not always been regress.

There is a chance, not to be missed, to present a very fresh vision of a 21st century health care system, in place of a 19th century one which has been trying to cope with 20th century diseases.

Overall, the over-arching concept should be the creation of a true public health system, in which medical care and medical professionals are a co-operative part. In place of the idea of omniscient medicine, the emphasis must be on examination of results, on broader co-operation within medicine, and between medicine, community and social care. Evidence, research and the critical absorption of new knowledge are much more central than new equipment. A return to the general practitioner or family doctor requires the enhancement of their status, at the expense of hospitals. The same is true of the need to create a true nursing profession. All of this cannot be controlled by a new 'managerial' group, but requires social control. (Such social control is much better exercised at the local government level.) In the end, then, a successful health care system thrives best where there is democracy, greater equality, and an emphasis on education. Individuals do need to take personal responsibility for much of their health, but the vast body of new evidence underscores the social foundations of good health. Public responsibility thus enhances individual responsibility in health care.

Specific recommendations are:

- Attention should be focused first on what kind of health care is needed. Once this debate is addressed properly, the question of how to fund that health care, and what can and should be afforded, makes sense.

- In terms of the efficient utilisation of given financial resources, there is no apparent advantage to social insurance or 'Bismarck' systems over the Swedish or British 'Beveridge' system of funding through taxation.

- Whilst there are serious constraints on funding for these, middle-income, countries, the most important problem is in assuring the greater efficiency of the existing systems. A high-quality, high morale group of health professionals is central to this process. Attempting to 'managerialise' instead, for cost containment, is not a recipe for success.

- Within this framework, the development of a high quality nursing profession and a high standard and morale for family and general practitioners is critical. The concept of the professional nurse should be central to new developments in the hospital sector in particular.

- The family or general practitioner can be an effective 'gatekeeper' to other medical services, and thus a good cost-controller. The use of doctors in this way to ration medical care, including pharmaceuticals, is never easy. It is, however, preferable to the situation where medical care costs do the rationing. In the case of ordinary drugs, rationing by price may not just be inequitable, but, by allowing the worsening of existing illnesses, will also be inefficient.

- To continue to improve health services, adequate funding is necessary, no matter what efficiency gains can be realised. Given the general problems of tax compliance in the region, an 'hypothecated tax', collected expressly for health spending, makes a great deal of sense. Where new social insurance systems appear to perform this function of making payment less unpopular, and have been implemented successfully, energy is undoubtedly better spent on other aspects of reform. But in those countries where financing reform has not been successful to date, serious consideration must be given to maintaining a 'Beveridge' system, with hypothecated taxes supplying extra finance where this is clearly in line with the country's ability and desire to pay.

- It is important to de-emphasise the highly technical specialist. Of course health care systems must satisfy the people, even though this may sometimes mean that objective evaluation would give different 'economic' answers. Health care reform should necessarily be incremental, but a vision will drive the best reforms. It will necessarily reflect long-standing national attitudes as well as new ideas gleaned from international experience. It is especially in the latter, and in evaluating what works and does not, that economists have a special role to play. To do this correctly, they also need to make their results comprehensible to the public.

There is much that can be done. There are no quick fixes, but there are many opportunities for immediate and visible gains that will create a further constituency for reform. The population also needs long-term assurance that its basic health care needs will be met, no matter what system of finance and organizational structure is put into place. In the reform debate, the need for this assurance is frequently lost.

Endnotes

1. For the higher income minority of the population excluded from the social insurance system for medical care, there are competing insurance companies in the Netherlands. However, in order to preserve solidarity, they are legally prevented from terminating policies with individual policyholders who pay their premiums (for example those with a high claims record) and in addition all private 'insurance' premiums include a sum used to subsidise the medical costs of elderly people. In a pure insurance market, medical premiums would increase with age and be a very high proportion of income for those over 80 – or be completely unaffordable.
2. A poorly-designed reform was introduced in Poland on 1 January 1999 and promptly provoked massive protest by health workers, including doctors. The outcome remains undetermined.

4. Housing

Housing and social policy

The problem of housing must be considered in two distinct ways, both of which are vitally important for social policy.

First, housing is a basic, critical commodity for everyone, the quality and affordability of which contributes a great deal to welfare. Even at this level, it should be clear that housing is 'not just bricks and mortar' (Oxley and Smith 1996). Well-designed housing aids health, badly-designed housing injures it (OECD 1996). Even something as simple as the design of the kitchen area vitally enhances, or detracts, from family living. Obviously the space and calm afforded by housing, and the local amenities, contribute a great deal to the individual quality of life.

In the countries of central and eastern Europe there is a general consensus that before transition housing was unsatisfactory, though affordable. It was short in quantity and worse in quality. For the most part the situation has deteriorated in the past decade. Nevertheless, it will be concluded in this chapter that housing need is not a major priority for social policy in most transition countries. The perceived housing shortage – for all but young families – is actually somewhat illusory in most countries. It was based on apparent demand, in a situation where rental costs and utility charges were very low by world standards. In fact, in the light of international comparisons, most transition countries do not have poorer quality and quantity of housing than their per capita GDP would indicate as normal. There are acute specific problems of creating a new housing market and homes for young families. There is also the need to make housing available in a way that will facilitate the migration that is critical for employment, removing the barriers created by labour market geographical mismatch. There is also an acute dilemma posed in the adjustment period to a housing policy which appropriately reflects the true cost of housing: whether to develop a system of housing and utility allowances and benefits (this is the general trend), and thus to increase the marginal rate of implicit taxation on the poor and accentuate the poverty trap, or whether to spread an effective subsidy across a wide group, in a situation where the fiscal constraints are already very tight. These latter questions are the key ones today. The development of an equitable and enabling policy towards mortgage markets, and even the encouragement of a dynamic private construction sector, are issues for which longer-term planning is appropriate, not swift (and perhaps expensive) 'emergency' measures.

It now seems quite bizarre that US bilateral aid was used until August 1998 to set up a mortgage programme for the middle-class of Moscow. Of course, in Prague or Budapest the issues are different, but here too there must be some serious thinking about priorities. Housing as investment is not the optimum way for a country to consider convergence with western Europe. It may well divert savings and other financial flows which would lead to more rapid economic growth if invested in other sectors, and thus, after some years, to a much better housing situation overall. Such deferred gratification in housing has characterised many successful growth spurts around the world (for example, the Japanese and the Swedish post-war experiences).

Individual consumption is only half of the housing question. If housing were, basically, a commodity like any other, there might be little justification for state intervention in the housing market as such. If an identifiable group of people could not afford the minimum standard of housing that the majority deems to be the present norm that could and should be assured, then perhaps (the problem of the poverty trap aside), the answer lies in income support and redistribution. This will be discussed below.

Housing, is also, however, the fundamental unit in which society lives, especially in urban settlements. In western Europe, it has been learned, to great cost, that poor overall strategies for housing, transport and jobs have been one of the causes of what is now termed 'social exclusion', one of the most corrosive and self-replicating problems (OECD 1996). It is this aspect, often called 'urban policy' (see Heidenheimer, Heclo and Adams 1983, for a still valuable overview) which has been seriously neglected in the transition. Across the region the problem of crime is identifiable as one of the most disturbing growth phenomena of the transition, and there is little serious policy debate and research about it. Western research indicates that an integrated consideration of housing, job opportunities, transport and other urban amenities is a key to avoiding what the omnibus term social exclusion has come to mean: the creation of a substantial group of people alienated from the rest of society, characterised not just by high crime rates (often most of all against others in the excluded group), and high unemployment and poverty, but also by the reproduction of these conditions (Weisbrod and Worthy 1997; OECD 1996). Whilst the cities of the old regimes were not ideal egalitarian socialist communities (Smith 1989), the new situation has dramatically increased the potential for the creation of such unpleasant and deteriorating urban environments. Housing policy is, therefore, a critical area for consideration for some forms of state action to avoid the social costs involved in the problems of urban inner cities and continental deprived suburbs. This is the time to consider how to avoid such conditions, because 'path-dependence' is critical in these perverse cycles of disadvantage.

Both these aspects of housing policy, 'individual' and 'social', raise important issues in the transition.

What has happened?

In the past decade housing construction in central and eastern Europe has collapsed, and collapsed far more than have industrial output or GDP.

This dramatic fall is a very visible illustration of the economic consequences of the 'institutional hiatus' in the region (UNECE, 1997a). The old state structures are gone and the necessary alternatives, private or social, do not yet exist. As a consequence, even in the best-placed countries, housing construction has nearly halved, and in others the fall has been to one-quarter the 1989 level. In the more successful reforming countries the bottom has now been reached. In some countries like Belarus there has been a (perhaps one-off) spurt. In others the situation remains stagnant. It is often thought that there is more housing construction than is officially recorded. This may certainly be true for housing starts. But experts believe that there is much less under-counting of completed and occupied dwellings.

Despite the collapse in construction, there is no apparent crisis. The reason is that the decline in the flow of new housing does not immediately make a great dent in the stock of available housing. This is an obvious feature of housing as a commodity: it is a very durable consumer good. The short-run elasticity of supply of the housing stock is thus everywhere unavoidably low. Additionally, as birth-rates throughout the region have also dropped sharply, even in the most successful economies such as Slovenia, and household incomes have been hard hit, there is, as yet, low effective demand for housing on the part of average citizens in central and eastern Europe.

New residential construction should not at this time be a major priority in social policy for any transition country. This might be surprising to many who have been hearing for a very long time about the deficiencies of the region's housing. The deficiencies are undeniable. Poor quality and an objective shortage – an excess of households over dwellings – are very real in a number of transition countries. There are, however, considerable national variations and in some cases the alleged need for new construction was created by the economic policies pursued. Where housing was allocated by the state, and rents were very low, there was, of course, persistent excess demand. Now, much of this perceived physical shortage has been turned into a shortage of affordable housing. Expanding supply overall is not the first way forward in this situation. Moreover, quality is generally a more serious problem than quantity.

Poland and Russia, for example, have marked objective housing stock deficits. More generally, in eastern Europe and the Baltic States there are only about 20 square metres of useful floor space per person, and only 16.4 square metres per person in the Russian Federation. As a broad generalisation, space provision is about half average western European levels (European Commission, 1995). Income, however, is not at all at western European levels either. Perhaps it is more surprising, then, that Hungarians and Estonians already have the same per capita housing space as Italians. Central and eastern European capitals are provided with per capita housing which is more generous than one would expect, given per capita incomes.

Steps certainly can and should be made to create a normal property market. This has turned out to be much more difficult than was at first envisioned. However, prioritising mortgages is not a sensible priority in the present circumstances, and is much more likely to benefit those who have already found themselves to be relative winners in the transition process. Why should there, for example, be a state subsidy in Slovakia for those whose personal savings have enabled them to borrow from the newly created (1992) building societies? The savings thus mobilised are not then going into much-needed investment in productive capacity.

What are the most urgent problems in housing?

If 'housing shortage' is not the issue at present, what are the real problems that need addressing? There are four critical areas: (a) quality; (b) problems of present cost relative to income, which in turn leads to (c) a serious limitation on labour mobility; and (d) the present flight from social housing which poses a long-term threat to social cohesion.

Addressing these economic and technical questions is made more difficult by an inadequate legal infrastructure that needs urgent renovation. For example, with respect to multi-family dwellings condominium legislation lags far behind what is needed to facilitate repair and improvement on a serious scale. A major difficulty is 'deferred maintenance'. This is the common regional euphemism for serious deterioration of multi-unit housing, which often came into the world already in need of major repairs. Ignoring the need for repairs today will carry the most serious long-run penalties. There are only broad indicators as to the magnitude and rate of increase of this problem. For example, in Budapest estimates of the cost of needed repairs range between 250 and 600 billion forints, or $1.7 billion to $4 billion. If deferred maintenance is not addressed across the board, then there will be increasing housing segregation, as flight occurs from the worst areas, and young families find only dilapidated property in which to settle. It must be recognised, of course, that it may simply not be reasonable to repair some badly-designed and poorly-maintained property, yet the costs of demolition are also immense.

Energy efficiency

The inherited housing stock is also in desperate need of improved energy efficiency. Utilities costs are a major burden on poorer families and on governments, and are usually higher than rents that allow for some physical maintenance. 'Retro-fits', undertaken under international pilot programmes have turned out to be both technically feasible and economically attractive. But the shortage of capital for all purposes is a major barrier to turning these pilot schemes into serious programmes, as is the scarcity of institutions that would organise the necessary work Exploring the opportunities for energy efficiency is not just an environmental, but a social priority, that has been lost in the maze of unclear jurisdiction and the immediate 'firefighting' of fiscal stringency. The full cost of utilities and housing maintenance is as high as 30 to 40 per cent of average household income in the Baltic countries and the CIS, and also in Poland, and not much lower elsewhere. A survey found that low-income Lithuanian households were spending 20 per cent of their monthly income (and 26 per cent in winter) on energy bills alone. Around 73 per cent of households stated that they had financial problems paying for energy.

The unattractive choice which this presents is that either across the board subsidies continue to be paid, a major financial burden on local government and/or the utilities themselves, or the currently fashionable means-tested housing subsidies are extended, despite the fact that they have proven to be one of the major sources of the 'poverty trap' and disincentives to work in countries such as Britain, which have already introduced them and experienced their effects. Indeed, such 'targeted' allowances might even be a disincentive to participate in energy-saving measures, if their payment is effectively capped.

Yet it would appear that with the right technology, will and organisation, there is much that can be done that is technically and economically feasible to reduce these high costs, and limit the need for subsidies, whether across-the-board or means-tested. The pilot projects that have been carried out, primarily with World Bank and bilateral aid, have shown an encouraging picture, if the institutional and financial barriers can be overcome. Of course, there are an immense number of variables that can affect the outcomes, ranging from labour and material costs to unexpected technical hitches. For example, a Finnish Energy Conservation Group project in Petrozavodsk (Karelia, Russia) estimated that heat control and substation changes to a five-storey, 60-flat building costing $25,000 per building would have a payback period of only four years. In a more extensive package, a complete overhaul in a Tallinn, Estonia project of the same size, the energy savings would be 30 to 50 per cent – depending on whether the heat supply in the building would be partially 'calibrated' (reduced). The cost would be $170,000 and the payback period from 7 to 14 years. There are about 40 similar projects, some pilot, some prospective, on which the World Bank has produced an impressive study summarising this experience. It concludes that, 'There are large technical opportunities to improve the energy efficiency of multifamily residential buildings with attractive financial returns'.

The barriers, as the report itself stresses, are not technical. In the present environment, it would seem implausible that anybody other than an agency (or local government agencies) charged with oversight on this issue could lead the way. As the latter are now the bodies who have to provide the bulk of the utility subsidies, they also have a material interest in undertaking this task. Financial support for domestic energy saving is an attractive area for foreign assistance programmes (both bilateral and multilateral). The benefits are both financial and social.

The confused legal infrastructure is an additional barrier to energy-saving capital improvement, as are the difficulties of disentangling obligations in district heating systems. The district heating systems have never been able to fulfil their great promise in the absence of any economic incentives for efficiency. The worst situation is to be found in the former Soviet Union, where low energy prices have been the background for massive distortions.

In some countries, notably in the Baltic states and Poland, there is already a quality turnaround, with growth in repair and renovation helping to offset the decline in housing starts (ECE 1998). Many of the problems of the existing housing stock demand innovative measures, using the best of international experience on how to refurbish badly-built housing.

Is there a case for state intervention?

The retreat from social housing is a striking fact throughout central and eastern Europe. Although existing rents in the remaining public sector are still often low, entry possibilities have been sharply reduced. This means that, in general, it has become very difficult to get into the social housing sector. The difficulty of entry is also a serious constraint on labour mobility, thus adding to the problems of labour market geographical mismatch, and increasing long-term unemployment.

The fiscal constraints that encouraged the flight from social housing are clear. The recipe which has been advocated, notably first by the World Bank, should, however, be carefully reconsidered. The Bank suggests that in place of social housing there should be income subsidies for the very poorest, and, in the end, market rents. In the difficult economic situation and the exceptional fiscal constraint prevailing across the region, this seems to make sense. The retreat from social housing is in line with the prevailing ethos. But is this new, broader-than-Washington consensus recipe of market rents, extensive housing allowances and (perhaps) mortgage subsidies really efficient?

In western industrialised economies housing represents more than a quarter of tangible capital wealth. Private households generally spend about 20-25 per cent of their income on housing. New housing construction represents between three and eight per cent of GDP (ECE, 1998b, pvii). State intervention in the housing market is all pervasive. Moreover,

> In most western European countries, in the absence of such intervention, something of the order of a quarter to a third of the total population would be unable to pay the full economic cost of the housing it occupies. (McCrone and Stephens, 1995, p2).

Yet there is no agreed view on why there is extensive public intervention, and if it is the right policy. In this respect housing economics lags behind that for the health care sector.

The reality of western European state involvement in housing is not widely recognised in central and eastern Europe. It is a powerful *prima facie* case for intervention: all successful social market economies have chosen to do it. Even in Hong Kong, 50 per cent of the population remains in social housing. This argument must, however, be handled with care. It might be that it is a universal but mistaken impulse, similar to that for agricultural subsidies. Some stalwart and sophisticated defenders of the efficiency of the welfare state have taken this tack. Thus Nicholas Barr has argued that equity is the main problem in the housing market, and that if equity is the main concern, then income transfers are most likely to be the best answer. The failures in social housing policy in Britain, seen through this prism, are 'predictable consequences of price subsidies introduced mainly to increase equity'. (Barr, 1998, p399).

Is equity really the driving force? Is it just compassion (or politics) that lie behind a desire to ensure that everyone has a 'decent home at a price they can afford', even subsidising this so that they consume more (or better) housing than they might choose if there were simply income transfers?

The significant feature that sets housing apart in a critical way is that externalities are pervasive. That is, there are significant third party effects. This obvious fact has led virtually all industrialised societies to impose zoning and planning regulations. That is not, however, the end of the matter. Even relatively distant housing can be the fertile soil for crime, unemployment and alienation, imposing massive social costs. The externalities of a slum on the other side of the city may therefore be very large. This fact first became evident in Britain in 1842 as a result of a cholera epidemic, before the microbiology of cholera was understood. Slums had 'miasmas' which could spread up the hill. The social miasma of modern slums is no less real.

Hence it is desirable to encourage others to consume better housing, at the expense in part of society as a whole. The alternative was clearly explained by Della Nevitt: 'The free market has always provided housing at a price people can afford. Such housing is called slums'. Houses are 'not just bricks and mortar', but the building blocks of neighbourhoods, communities and cities. Western research is revealing the link between poor housing and crime, poor housing and unemployment. A blithe indifference to geographical and housing tenure stratification is potentially disastrous, injurious to social cohesion and destructive of equality of opportunity. It is therefore beneficial to society as a whole if people have better housing than they might be able to afford, and even than, if offered income, they might voluntarily choose. The efficient level of housing is thus higher than the market alone might provide.

In central and eastern Europe, to a far greater degree than in the west, the escalation of crime has resulted in a high sense of public insecurity. Whilst there is much that can, should, and is being done to encourage modern policing and probation services, the evidence from the United States and western Europe over several decades indicates the limits of this approach, and, importantly, strongly suggests that the spatial distribution of crime in urban areas, and its growth, owe much to the operation of the housing market which has given rise to what have been termed marginalisation and 'residualisation'. The latter means that some areas, and housing tenures, have become increasingly the place for 'leftovers', those without strong links to the labour market or to others in the community, in short the socially excluded (OECD 1996a). Housing geography has yet another link to rising crime levels, as spatial mismatch exacerbates unemployment or non-employment that in turn increases crime rates in a number of ways. The inhabitants of the 'residualised' areas are, of course, also disproportionately the victims of crime, but developments in the United States, where two per cent of males of working age are presently in prison, have also demonstrated that an attempt at crime containment through geographical polarisation is both remarkably expensive and will not contain crime. Thus policies which contain or reverse processes leading to geographic segregation are not only equitable, but when successful are also efficient.

The housing changes which produced the American and British inner cities, and are now represented in the marginalized areas of continental western Europe, did not happen overnight, but over decades. The changes in the social landscape of the countries in transformation will also be gradual. The long time period involved provides the opportunity of avoiding what has been described as one potential 'time bomb', the transformation of housing estates on the peripheries of cities into classic slums. This involves, however, a concerted programme including labour market and transportation measures as well as housing maintenance and social services. In some areas, such as greater Budapest, there is a very different process of social stratification taking a sharp spatial form, that of suburbanisation – the desertion of the cities by the better off. This continues a trend that commenced just before the beginning of transition.

An economic upturn could begin to replicate the conditions of the American inner city 'ghetto' in Budapest. The 8th and 9th districts of Budapest have for two to three decades begun to develop the necessary preconditions for such a status. (This draws attention yet again to the importance, and effects, of 'deferred maintenance'.) Whilst previously social segregation in Budapest did indeed result in the residential concentration of high-income groups, the classic patterns of western sociology did not yet fit the low status groups. Marginalization of the poor was limited to small areas. Hungary's new economic growth will enhance the pull to Budapest, particularly of the poor at present trapped in rural and peripheral slums. On this scenario, there could be a repetition of a classic pattern, beginning with upper-middle class departure from the inner city. The middle class, which has not yet been enriched enough to follow suit, might feel impelled to do so in turn.

This, however, is a particularly dramatic example. The weight and role of Budapest, the largest city of east-central Europe, with one fifth of the country's population, is unique. It differs, therefore from that of other capital cities and also from smaller cities and new towns. Here too, the most skilled workers and the intelligentsia have long been relatively favourably housed, but the fate of less advantaged areas and deteriorating inner cities – whether or not they will become classic slums – remains to be determined. A successful non-market housing sector, of whatever institutional form, requires civic consciousness and not just competent management. Once an area has been residualised, recovery becomes a very difficult task. Prevention is much cheaper than cure, but does require the interest, concern, foresight, and political and administrative capacity, to respond to the failings of the market mechanism.

Another aspect of the relationship between spatial differentiation and social stratification in Hungary concerns the increasing consciousness of the large rural population of being trapped in dead-end villages. In Hungary in the 1980s, 35 per cent of the population still lived in rural settlements, though only one quarter of them were engaged in farming as their primary occupation. These villages, even those close to metropolitan areas, and in relatively prosperous Hungary, have in a number of cases very poor infrastructure (no telephones, sewage disposal or even running water).

In Warsaw the process of spatial differentiation seems to have taken a somewhat more benign path, in part because of the increasing concentration of the elderly in central districts, which has been going on for a long time. The marginalisation of the elderly poor has strong equity implications, but does not generate concerns about increases in crime, unemployment and social tension. The creation of a housing market has, naturally, encouraged subletting. The process of gentrification of desirable areas, on the one hand, and marginalisation of undesirable ones on the other, seems to be far less advanced than in Budapest.

In the same way in which the capital cities have dominated the economic and political landscape, they seem also to have dominated the study of urban and housing change in the region. What has happened to spatial and social stratification in the smaller cities is less clear.

A further reason, owing as much to equity as efficiency, why there is often a social preference for ensuring that housing meets certain minimum standards, is that children do not choose their own housing. For reasons of individual and social development it is important that children grow up in physical conditions that meet certain minimum standards and in a socially integrated environment.

So for the overall social health of societies, housing segregation should be minimised. This contributes to minimising educational segregation, without requiring the end of neighbourhood schools. Housing segregation by social class and income group is a major barrier to equality of opportunity. It is a proven risk factor in social conflict, crime and unemployment. Once again, simple market provision will not give the most efficient outcome. It is quite possible that if higher income households are persuaded that they do not wish to assist in improving housing for poorer sections of society that they will wish to provide neighbourhood services privately, and to remove themselves physically from problem neighbourhoods and 'dump estates'. The American 'gated community', from which residents must drive through streets where carjacking is a real threat, is an extreme end-result of this trend. While central and eastern European cities have had good and bad neighbourhoods, attractive housing and poor estates, the extremes of the United States have so far been avoided. It would be foolish to go down this ultimately expensive road in the name of fiscal stringency.

Homelessness in Central and Eastern Europe

Since the start of the transformation, homelessness has emerged as a new and significant social problem. Although homelessness existed also under the old regime, it was much less visible. People who did not have a fixed abode (often they were unemployable alcoholics, itinerant labourers or ex-prisoners) were persecuted by the police and imprisoned. The USSR practiced particularly severe persecution for 'violation of [internal] passport rules', 'systematic vagrancy and begging' and for so-called 'long-term parasitic way of life'. Other countries in the Soviet bloc also had legal persecution for 'work avoidance'.

Prior to the transformation, the problem of homelessness was not officially recognised. Secular and church-run homeless-assistance institutions were closed (in the USSR in the 1920s and in eastern Europe in the 1950s). Even today in many of the countries of the region there is no official recognition of the problem of homelessness.

The current numbers of the homeless in central and eastern Europe remain uncertain. This is partly because of definitional difficulties, and partly because of the absence of reliable large-scale surveys. Some surveys suggest that the numbers are substantial, especially in capital cities that attract migrants. It has been estimated that there are currently 55,000 homeless people in St.Petersburg and 100,000 in Moscow. In Budapest, where the homeless are also very visible, their number is currently estimated at about 18,000-20,000.

The very visible increase in the number of homeless is partly a result of a decrease in police repression. This is a positive result of the transformation process. Partly, however, it is a result of changes in the housing and labour markets, and more generally of a widespread weakening of social integration. These changes have had a particularly negative effect on individuals who are already marginalised, due to family circumstances, recent (forced) migration, alcohol or drug consumption, or prison records. Among these changes are:

- The closing of workers' hostels;
- Elimination or reduction of institutional housing (mental hospitals, state orphanages, reformatories for alcoholics);
- High cost of housing relative to wages (this problem is particularly acute for divorced men, who cannot afford to rent housing after a family break-up);
- Loss of housing in property frauds (particularly in Russia in 1991-97 in connection with housing privatisation – many of the victims were elderly people or alcoholics);
- The increasing number of evictions for non-payment of rent;
- A sharp decrease in employment and housing opportunities for ex-prisoners who also lost their homes or never had ones;
- Increase in regional differentiation of unemployment rates leading to extensive migration to areas with relatively low unemployment rates;
- Forced migration from areas of wars and/or ethnic conflicts;
- Growth of the number of street children and young people. These typically come from low-income families, with precarious employment and parental alcohol problems. Such families have found themselves during the transformation under enormous strains from the increase in inequality, explosion of poverty, decline of employment and growth of unemployment, and erosion of traditional male roles. Children and youths often take to the streets to escape violence and abuse and try to earn their living independently (often by theft as in Dickensian London)

As a response to the problem of homelessness, the countries of the region are developing institutions of social assistance, including hostels and shelters. Many official efforts, however, are still centred round persecution and harassment of street people. The Russian police are particularly brutal in their treatment of the homeless. There are numerous reports from Russia of homeless people being dumped at rubbish tips or forests outside city boundaries. Strict residency rules in some Russian cities (which are applied despite the fact that they have been declared illegal by the courts) often prevent the homeless getting legal jobs or even access to welfare provisions such as unemployment benefits or pensions.

The peculiarities of housing and the choice of policies

Housing is a very durable commodity. The short-run elasticity of supply is very low, as the flow of new housing is a small proportion of the historically acquired stock. Serious change must necessarily be gradual.

Housing is very expensive relative to income. This implies that a developed capital market will be required, particularly for owner-occupation, and a solid legal structure. Such developments have never emerged spontaneously. A range of financial institutions has been developed specific to the problems of this sector. The variation between countries is large, as is the degree of implicit or explicit subsidy involved. Mortgages are not an appropriate target for state subsidy, on either equity or efficiency grounds, but establishing the framework for good mortgage markets is a desirable area for active public policies. Historical evidence suggests that the mortgage market usually suffers from market failure, because of risk, information asymmetry, or the excess of the private over the social rate of time preference. Historically, housing finance markets have been given a strong impetus by state action in developed countries. The subsidies for owner-occupation have had perverse distributional results. They have often been the result of political competition for precisely the most politically mobile 'floating voters' in the prosperous working class. However, some institutional guarantees from the state have been exceptionally beneficial in promoting wider access to better housing, by minimising risk, at little direct cost.

Housing is special in that it is quite inflexible – the costs of alteration are quite high. It is fixed in location, and location is very important. Houses are also homes. The link between housing and transport can be very important for employment. Here again atomised market decisions will almost certainly not provide the optimal result.

The failure of unassisted markets to meet fundamental efficiency conditions implies that strong consideration should be given to some form of state involvement, though this, of course, is subject to the possibility of state failure. In the new civil societies of the region, it may be harder than usual to launch new forms of social housing, but this is an important way forward where possible. Well-run cooperatives and housing associations have been instrumental in improving housing in many western European countries. The past character of many central and east European cooperatives has naturally provoked a negative reaction in the present. It is possible this reaction will not be long-lived, as a new generation comes on to the housing market. In any event, the legislative framework should be put in place where it is not already, and secured where it has been inadequately launched.

To sum up this section: as housing is expensive, and particularly given the pervasive externalities, many people will not be able to afford the minimum standards of housing which the majority wants society to have. This, combined with the fact that children do not choose their own accommodation, is arguably the underlying rationale for this internationally widespread form of what are effectively benefits-in-kind (even if in the form of housing allowances). Housing is, however, more than a roof over one's head. Housing is the physical infrastructure for society. Reduction of the housing issue to an income issue misses what is unique and critical about the sector. If housing is not approached with a view to minimising social exclusion, then the worst features of North American cities can quickly be replicated. This involves not only high unemployment in the excluded areas, but a situation in which young people growing up do not even know anyone who has a job. It is a proven breeding ground for crime, already the most painful growth product in central and eastern Europe.

There is a substantial and weighty case for public intervention in the housing market since this is an area where markets fail to take account of all the relevant costs and benefits. As housing policy has never been built up as a single coherent whole, this reasoning is a form of reverse engineering. Housing policy everywhere is complex, often messy, and consists of an elaborate patchwork of measures. The rational economist is understandably irritated by this untidy, historically accumulated, tangle. Yet, as John Hills (1991) warned, the evidence is clear that the way to untangle a cat's cradle is *not* to find the best available loose end and tug. This is as true for central and east European housing as it is for the British case.

The first tug, privatisation, has failed to produce the desired results, and the next tug is getting more insistent – a drive across the region to raise rents, in combination with the enhancement of housing allowances. Is this sensible? It appears to meet the conditions for enhancing housing consumption on the part of the poorest sections of the population. It is appealing in central and eastern Europe because fiscal constraints make talk of 'targeting' extremely attractive. However, as has been argued in Chapter 1, and will be examined further in Chapter 6 below, the central dilemma is that all such targeting provides a serious disincentive to work. The effective marginal tax rate for low-income families seeking to improve their situation may be close to – or in extreme cases, as a result of a multiplicity of income-related benefits, even above – 100 per cent. Moreover, the provision of housing allowances for those who then purchase or rent in a free market may result, if the elasticities are unfavourable, in an increase in prices or a 'capitalisation' of subsidies into land or house prices, without much improvement in housing for the subsidised consumer. This is simply a waste of public money.

Housing policies and inevitable trade-offs

The historically low rents (and low wages) of central and eastern Europe are well known, famously including the fact that Russian rents did not rise from 1926 to mid-1994. Not just rentals are involved, but rather all charges, including utilities. One strong motive for élite support for privatisation was surely the hope that these costs could somehow be shifted by the magic of ownership change. As Turner argued with respect to Estonia, the transfer from enterprise to underdeveloped municipality, and thence to the citizens, has resembled less the transfer of an asset, and more that of a hot potato (Turner, 1996).

Early in the transition process the World Bank and USAID proposed that housing charges should cover costs, if not yet approach market rates. As many tenants would not be able to pay these charges without spending the bulk of their income on them, it was proposed that a system of housing allowances should be introduced. Everyone owes a full-cost rent. Those for whom it would be more than a certain proportion of disposable income would receive a deduction so that the proportion of the income they paid in rent would be capped. This policy mix is already operating in some countries, notably Ukraine and the Czech Republic.

Housing allowances, under normal conditions, seem a workable measure. It is especially appropriate to cushion the shock of raising rents. There are, however, a number of inherent defects and trade-offs. As the British Treasury has found to its dismay, this sort of housing benefit is an alarmingly open-ended commitment. And if not gradually tapered it provides the usual disincentive to work. It should be emphasised that these disincentive effects are still highly debateable, and emotion has often been substituted for evidence. Yet it seems reasonable to argue that such measures have a cumulative disincentive effect. Few drop out of the labour market, feigning disability or unemployment, just because of this 'poverty trap'. But once misfortune – illness, job loss, marital breakdown – occurs, the incentive to return, or to seek a more demanding job, is understandably diminished.

The argument against over-enthusiastic embrace of housing allowances goes beyond the question of disincentives. Wages in most central and eastern European countries are still low by west European standards. Building in housing allowances at this stage is actually crystallising the old low-rent, low-wage regime. A better time for introducing anything but temporary patches is surely when recovery is strong. In the most fiscally pressed states, such as the Russian Federation, there is the further dilemma that even the middle-income groups are scarcely well-off in absolute terms. There is thus a very hard trade-off indeed. Once again this suggests that if there are housing allowances, they need to be quite gradually tapered.

A serious argument for the rent increase plus housing allowance scheme is the regressive nature of the allocation of housing, with higher income groups enjoying the best housing. Yet it is *not* as unequally distributed as money income, and historically has been, on balance, an equalising factor. Buckley and Gurenko (1997) estimate that in 1992 the housing component reduced the Gini coefficient in Russia from 41.7 to 35.4, a very large reduction indeed. Much care and empirical work are needed to establish the nature of housing subsidies as regressive or progressive, not just to insist on their nature from *a priori* considerations.

It is also important to choose a sensible housing policy. This is a potentially vast sector, with serious macroeconomic impact. There is a great deal of enthusiasm for the starter-motor benefit of housing at the moment, so a final word of caution is in order: a society can promote housing consumption to its detriment too. Housing finance does compete for funding with other investment. An open-minded and a cautious approach may not sound so fine as sloganeering, but in the longer run real improvement in housing – for individuals and as an essential social framework – will best be attained in central and eastern Europe if there is not an unnecessary emphasis on improving all housing, ahead of economic growth. The emphasis should, instead, be on removing the worst problems.

Re-orienting housing policy

In western Europe housing policy is today undergoing substantial reform. The efficiency of high levels of housing subsidies in countries such as Sweden and Denmark, amounting to three to five per cent of

GDP, is being questioned (Turner, 1996). In central and eastern Europe, however, the neo-liberal overshoot with its crudely simplified economics has posed the wrong questions. Sadly, the agenda has been set by an issue that, even by one of its most articulate proponents (Struyk, 1996, pp22-3), is acknowledged to be essentially ideological, the symbolic privatisation of the existing stock of public housing.

Privatisation of housing was grasped as one more weapon in the battle to make the transition to capitalism irreversible. At the time this seemed a much more urgent task than it may in retrospect, and *ex ante* worthy of more sacrifice than *ex post*. The most illogical outcome of this has been in the Russian Federation, where the implications of ownership of a flat have been very fuzzy indeed, especially when the privatisation begins only at the fortified door of the flat. Often this is in an inconvenient sprawling housing estate, still 'maintained' by a public organisation, with little apparent impetus for the creation of condominiums from the dwellings themselves. The ideological nature of this battle meant that social ownership alternatives to the state were simply not on the agenda, and it will very hard to argue for them now, even though some form of social ownership, or at any rate collective management, is highly appropriate to the type of housing stock (large blocks of flats).

The intensity of the privatisation wave in the region has been such that 'owner-occupation' in much of central and eastern Europe has not only caught up with, but outstripped western European levels. The data in Table 4.1 highlights another salient fact about housing that is often obscured: it is *not* the case that increased owner occupation is a feature of affluent countries. There are poor countries with high shares of owner occupation, and rich countries with quite modest levels of owner occupation.

Nor do the *ex ante* conditions suggest that state ownership was so pervasive as to justify making privatisation the focus for so long (see Table 4.2).

Of course the data in tables 4.1 and 4.2 are very aggregated. If just urban housing were considered, the proportion of owner occupied housing in the transition countries prior to reform would be reduced. Nevertheless, it remains difficult to see what was the housing (and non-political and non-ideological) case for rapid privatisation prior to adequate arrangements for maintenance and management of the common parts.

Table 4.1 Owner occupation

	Percentage of dwellings owner-occupied
Austria, 1994	53.5
Bulgaria, 1995	92.6
Estonia, 1995	61.3
Finland, 1994	62.1
Germany, 1993	38.8
Hungary, 1995	92.5
Latvia, 1995	41.3
Lithuania, 1995	88.9
Netherlands, 1994	47.6
Poland, 1995	56.4
Romania, 1995	92.4
Russian Federation, 1995	41.0
Turkey, 1994	70.5
United States, 1993	57.5

Source: UN/ECE Housing database, see UN/ECE 1997b, p136

Table 4.2 Tenure distribution of the housing stock prior to reform

	State rental	*Coop*	*Owner-occupied*	*Other*
Russian Federation, 1990	67	4	26	3
Armenia, 1980	53	4	43	-
Estonia	60	12	26	2
Bulgaria, 1985	16	-	84	-
Czech Republic, 1988	38	18	41	3
Hungary, 1990	23	6	71	-
Poland, 1990	35	25	40	-
Slovak Republic, 1988	25	20	53	2
Slovenia, 1981	33	-	67	-

Source: Struyk 1996

As with corporate privatisation, governance will emerge as a critical overlooked 'detail'. In the real front-runners, especially Slovenia (Mandic and Stanovnik, 1996) and Hungary (Hegedus, Mark and Tosics, 1996), that no longer have a crude excess of enumerated households over dwellings, the real second-generation issues of legal and institutional structure for housing finance will be more important. To flourish, the housing market requires supporting financial institutions. Housing, especially modern urban housing, usually costs a multiple of the annual income of a family. Housing built for rental has a substantial gestation period. If there is to be private finance, then there must be the development of financial institutions, backed by a strong legal framework. However, finance, and legislation, for housing improvement should have priority over the politically driven expansion of owner occupation.

Local government

In the development of urban programmes, and for all social policy, the continued development of local government remains a key priority. An effective and responsive welfare state is impossible without strong reliance on local government.

In central Europe there has been striking progress in the renewal of local government, both formal and de facto. Czech, Polish, and Hungarian laws, for example, guarantee the decentralisation of power. Local government requires, however, not just a legal basis, but also the appropriate resources. The degree of autonomy over resources at the local level remains in general relatively low, except in Poland where local taxes have been developed to the greatest extent. A steady, pragmatic, but consistent approach to the development of local government is necessary, as one can see by observing how long it has taken southern Europe to make its transition in this sphere. As each country has its own legacy, fiscal constraints, and geographical features, a 'one size fits all' model of local government is certainly not in order, but a concentration of reform efforts on this level of public administration certainly is.

Conclusions

- There is no quantity crisis that demands the large-scale diversion of resources into housing construction at this point.
- What is critical is the maintenance and improvement of the existing housing stock. Energy-efficient retro-fitting is possible and likely to be an important step on the road to sustainable development. The legal barriers preventing this – such as the absence of good condominium legislation – can be as important as capital shortages.

- There is no need for a 'jump-start' at this time. The urge to engage in political bidding for the middle sectors of society – through mortgage support in particular – can establish long-term regressive structures for which there is no justification.
- Caution should be exercised in rushing to a system of high 'market' rents sustained by housing allowances. This may deepen the poverty trap. Improvements in 'targeting' in this area may be especially damaging if they encourage further geographic segregation of differing social and income groups. A well-tapered system of allowances, and careful consideration for minimizing housing segregation must be part of the programme.
- A crisis mentality should be avoided. A long-term set of projections is needed, so that there can be broad democratic discussion, and so that it is clear that the issue has not been forgotten. Elaborate and demagogic promises should be avoided. An open and clear assessment can be a good substitute.
- The major area needing attention is the mechanism for repair, the assessment for what is to be done with housing which it does not seem economic to repair, and the improvement of sound but unattractive housing, especially on large estates. This is critical, too, for the question of housing policy as part of integrated urban policy.
- Increasing the energy efficiency of existing housing is an attractive investment opportunity that can reduce the burden of utility charges for many families.
- Homelessness has emerged as a significant social problem in a number of capital cities. It should be dealt with by the provision of hostels and shelters, not by police repression.
- In the longer run, with economic growth, housing will properly emerge as a major issue. By this time it is desirable for the legal and financial infrastructure to be in place. If social housing has not been reduced to 'dump estates', the prospects will be much brighter for an attractive package resembling the best west European experience.
- Although there may be no overall crisis, there is a definite need to improve the capacity of young families to enter the housing

market, and of the unemployed to move to where there are work opportunities. A good, if limited, social housing programme can fruitfully address these issues. It promises a higher return, and thus greater economic efficiency, than major programmes of housing benefit and higher rents, despite the promises made by their advocates.

- Housing policy is, at the moment, much more of a damage limitation exercise. The damage that should be limited is both physical and social. Physically it is the further decay of the inherited housing stock. Socially it is pervasive and stubborn social exclusion resulting from the free working of the market mechanism is the housing area. This potential damage is one of the greatest threats to welfare in the transition countries. The social damage that can result from poor housing policies is – unfortunately – already widely visible in North America and western Europe. The transition countries have the possibility of learning from this experience.
- The development of local government – which has already made good progress in central Europe – must play an important part in developing an effective and responsive housing policy.

5. Pensions

Pension reform issues in the 1990s

In all market economies there has been mounting concern about the sustainability of pension systems dominated by Pay As You Go (PAYG) arrangements, in which current pensions are paid out of current employee contributions. The problem arises from a combination of population ageing, aggravated by growing unemployment, and relatively high pensions with respect to the size and length of contributions. Declining fertility, after the post-War baby boom, and rising life expectancy, have raised dependency ratios, ie the number of old age pensioners per employee; such ratios, also known as support ratios, are poised to rise further in the medium term. The United Kingdom and Sweden show the least deterioration because of relative moderate increases in support ratios and the combination of pension benefits indexed to the CPI while contributions are geared to nominal wages. Also in the UK, PAYG provisions are much less important than elsewhere, as private funds were introduced earlier (see Chand and Jaeger 1996; Leibfritz, Roseveare, Fore and Wurzel, 1995).

In central and eastern European economies pensions figure even more prominently in the transition agenda (EC 1997b). In these economies there existed very broad social insurance systems, providing protection ‘from cradle to grave’. They included a pension system, which was part of the general budget and therefore regardless of formal arrangements equivalent to a PAYG system. Naturally pensions were subject to the same ‘soft constraints’ as all budgetary expenditures. Any current shortfall was automatically covered by the state budget. At the inception of the transition in central and eastern Europe, pensions amounted to between two thirds and three quarters of social security expenditures, and often were the largest single budgetary item, sometimes more than ten per cent of GDP.

The importance of pension reform in the transition economies is partly due to the same demographic and fiscal considerations relevant to market economies. Indeed, in some countries demographic trends have been exacerbated by initial, often sustained, falls in fertility (though mortality also rose, with uneven net effects). Table 5.1 illustrates retirement age, dependency ratios and the share of pension expenditures in GDP, in selected countries. Dependency ratios are worse than in OECD countries (as illustrated also in Table 5.2 indicating population structure and contributors per pensioner). The share of pension

Table 5.1 Public pension systems in transition economies (selected countries)

	Male retirement age[a]	*Demographic dependency ratio(%)*[b]	*System dependency ratio(%)*[c]	*Public pension expenditures (% of GDP)*	*Year*
Albania	-	17	37	5.9	1994
Armenia	65[d]	22	34	6.7	1994
Azerbaijan	60	19	-	4.7	1995
Belarus	60	33	49	10.3	1995
Bulgaria	60	37	87	8.0	1995
Czech Republic	60	32	52	6.7	1995
Estonia	60	32	52	6.7	1995
Georgia	60	30	45	11.0	1992
Hungary	60	20	34	2.4	1993
Kyrgyzstan	60	20	34	2.4	1993
Latvia	60	33	51	9.8	1995
Lithuania	60[e]	30	53	4.8	1994
Moldova	60	26	-	4.1	1994
Poland	60	28	49	14.6	1995
Romania	60	29	62	6.5	1993
Russian Fed	60	31	46	5.5	1993
Slovak Republic[f]	60	32	42	9.9	1995
Slovenia	-	29	54	13.7	1995
Ukraine	60	36	-	8.0	1993
Averages[g]					
Eastern Europe, Baltics and CIS	60.0	30.0	48.3	7.3	
Asia	55.5	15.3	11.4	1.9	
Latin America	60.8	14.9	21.0	2.0	
OECD Countries	64.4	32.9	39.2	9.2	

a 1991

b Number of people 60 and over divided by the number of those aged 20-59, 1990

c Ratio of current beneficiaries to contributors, public pension schemes, 1990

d 1996

e 1994

f Male retirement age, demographic dependency ratio and system dependency ratio refer to the former Czechoslovak Republic

g All averages are weighted except for the system dependency ratio of Asia, Latin America and OECD

Source: World Bank, IMF, OECD and national authorities, from World Development Report 1996.

expenditures in GDP is much higher than relative income levels with respect to OECD countries might have led one to expect. Pension benefits were relatively high because of low wages and low personal savings.

The budgetary implications of pension arrangements have become prominent in the generalised fiscal crisis and initial recession of early transition (Campbell and Owsiak, 1994). In the ten countries which are candidates for the first or even the second round of EU enlargement, a commitment to adoption of the *acquis communautaire* includes eventual EMU membership, so that failure to avoid or resolve the structural problems apparently created by current pensions arrangements might prejudice EU accession.

Table 5.2 Population structure and contributors per pensioner in selected transition economies, 1993

	Persons of working age per person 60+	*Contributors per pensioner*
Albania	7.9	1.0
Bulgaria	2.9	1.2
Czech Republic	3.5	2.0
Hungary	3.2	1.5
Poland	4.6	1.9
Romania	3.6	2.0
Russia	2.9	1.9
OECD average, 1990	3.6	2.6

Source: World Bank World Development Report 1996 p79

Four additional reasons for the importance of pension reform are specifically related to the transition:

- First, the switch from a state-run economy to an economy based predominantly on private ownership, which naturally suggests at least a partial switch from state to private provision of pensions.
- Second, the use of early retirement and disability pensions in order to ease the individual cost of downsizing uneconomic activities in the restructuring that accompanies the transition. In Bulgaria, for instance, the ratio of pensioners to employed workers, which had stood at 58 per cent in 1990, increased to 86 per cent in 1993, which was reflected in an increase in social

security benefits from 10.4 per cent of GDP in 1989 to 15.2 per cent in 1993 (Blanchard 1997). In Poland, from December 1989 to December 1993 the total number of pensioners increased by 28 per cent, from 6.9 to 8.8 million (Maret and Schwartz 1994). The corresponding burden on the state budget was not, therefore, entirely the legacy of the old system but also included some socialisation of the cost of transition. While pensioners have suffered in absolute terms in all transition economies, in many cases contrary to widespread perceptions they have suffered less, often significantly less, than the rest of the population, in particular children. For instance, in 1991-92 in Poland, old age pensioners while suffering a real income decline actually succeeded, paradoxically, in improving significantly their position relatively to wages.

- Third, the absence of any tradition of private pension provisions, as well as of other forms of private financial investments. In transition economies private provision for old age consisted solely of intra-family inter-generational solidarity, as in the rural areas of less developed countries.

- Fourth, the rise of unanticipated and unusual practices and outright abuses, in the course of transition. For instance, in Russia 'many observers allege that the pension fund and the social security funds were deposited in local banks in zero-interest deposits' (Warner 1997). In Russia and Ukraine, and in other FSU republics, the combination of non-affordable pensions and unattainable fiscal deficit targets (especially due to reduced ability to collect taxes) has led to large-scale pension arrears. In Belarus in 1997 a solvent pension system was pushed onto the verge of bankruptcy by a Presidential decree allowing state enterprises to postpone payment of their contributions (overwhelmingly larger than those of employees) without any allowance for interest or other penalty, with inflation eroding their real value at two to four per cent per month.

As a result of these general and transition-specific processes post-communist economies face the task of reforming or replacing all or part of their old PAYG (or PAYG-like) system. The PAYG system is deemed no longer affordable for a rapidly ageing population in the new environment of on-going macroeconomic stabilisation or newly found stability.

Just like market economies, transition economies are confronted with three basic reform options, which can be taken individually or combined in varying proportions:

- A financial tightening of the existing 'benefit-defined' PAYG system, in order to eliminate the burden on public finances or at least reduce it to a bearable level. This is the approach followed by Britain, Germany and Spain. Concretely it means a gradual increase in the retirement age and in social security contributions, greater flexibility in choosing the retirement age, incentives to postpone retirement beyond the normal age, lengthening the reference period for computing pensionable earnings, and reduction of the benefits accruing for each year of employment.
- The (at least partial) replacement of PAYG by a fully funded (FF) private and 'contributions-defined' system, whereby individual pensions are determined by lifetime contributions and by the yield on the assets they are used to buy. Effectively this involves the partial privatisation of social security. Examples of such policies may be found in Chile, Argentina, Mexico, the UK, and are under discussion in the US.
- An additional reform of the state-run PAYG system aimed at mimicking the link between individual pensions, the value of lifetime contributions, and life expectancy at retirement, without privatising pension provision (Italy, Sweden). A connection can also be established with the country's economic performance.

In addition, a voluntary pension tier can be promoted by public policy. This tier, in turn, may be split into a personal voluntary pension system and an occupational pension representing a contractual saving arrangement reached with employers. This is an important distinction in practice, as company pension schemes involve issues of 'portability' of pension rights across employers, state regulation and guarantees (which will not be discussed here). Technically, however, both voluntary and occupational pensions belong to the 'voluntary' pillar/tier and therefore no distinction will be drawn between them. The small capitalisation of pension funds in

Table 5.3 Pension funds (1996)[a]

	No of funds	*No of members (1000s)*	*Total assets % GDP*
Czech Republic	44	1125	0.14
Hungary	212	247	0.16
Russia	1,000	na	0.03
France			3.4
Germany			5.8
Italy			1.2
Japan			44.7
Switzerland			79.5
Netherlands			88.5
United Kingdom			79.4
United States			59.1

a End 1993 data for comparator countries

Source: EBRD Transition Report 1997

transition economies, especially relatively to advanced market economies, is well illustrated in Table 5.3.

As a result of these developments, all transition economies in the late 1990s are moving away from a one-tier (or pillar) PAYG system, duly reformed and scaled down, to a three-tier system with the addition of fully funded statutory and voluntary components. This chapter considers some general issues of pension systems; the implications of shifting from a PAYG to a funded pension system; and the intermediate alternative of mimicking some of the characteristics of full funding within a state-run PAYG. Policy recommendations are summarised at the end.

General issues

Private provision for the needs of the elderly takes two forms: (a) intra-family solidarity, whereby children look after their parents and any other old family members, effectively representing a form of insurance, and (b) individual savings and dis-savings over the life cycle, involving life insurance, annuities, as well as any other assets, including saving and pension schemes which may be set up voluntarily by employers and regulated by contract, with contributions which are a form of deferred earnings.

In modern economies the state intervenes in both kinds of private arrangements by introducing elements of compulsion.

Typically the state modifies intra-family solidarity by extending intergenerational solidarity from the family to society as a whole, with pensions paid to today's elderly generations over retiring age out of compulsory contributions made contemporaneously by younger generations currently employed. The ratio s = N/E between the number of current old age pensioners N and of current employees E is the support ratio or elderly dependency ratio (sometimes also expressed as a proportion of active population). This system is the so-called pay as you go (PAYG), or redistribution, pension system.

The state can impose or subsidise regular, individual savings out of income, channelled to a pension fund or funds, which provide a state pension and/or a private pension additional to other (if any) voluntary private provisions. This is the so called funded, or capitalisation, pension system. (Totally private funded pensions schemes are possible, but most existing funded pensions are normally encouraged, subsidised – eg by tax concessions – or imposed, by the state.)

A survivor's (or partner's) pension can be treated as an extension of the old age pensioner's life, usually at a reduced pension level. The longer life expectancy of women and hence higher incidence of women among survivors normally involves a transfer across genders. Within the standard PAYG system an additional transfer across genders results from the common practice of having an earlier retiring age for women than for men. A further cross subsidisation in favour of women may also exist in a PAYG system with uniform benefits but proportionate contributions, since women have both lower average earnings and lower participation rates than men. More generally, the standard PAYG system involves a considerable variability in the returns obtained by pensioners on their lifetime contributions, individually and, on average, across socio-demographic groups, genders and life-style groups (for example, smokers and non-smokers).

Disability can be regarded as forced early retirement, and can be modelled as an increase in the average dependency ratio under the PAYG regime, while it is covered by private insurance under the capitalisation system. Therefore survivor and disability pensions do not require a distinctive approach.

Naturally, state interference with private provision of resources for the elderly and the disabled has fiscal implications – whether through lower revenues due to tax exemptions on savings for old age, or through higher expenditure for direct contributions to pensions or savings under either system. Indeed historically the first pension systems (for tax-collectors, soldiers, and other state employees) were entirely funded out of taxation. Conceptually there is not much difference between compulsory contributions to a PAYG system (by employees and employers) and taxation. However, unlike other income transfers funded by taxation, tax-funded pensions involve not only the current fiscal stance but also a multi-annual policy commitment with obligations and claims vis-à-vis future pensioners and taxpayers.

Directly or indirectly, all pension regimes impinge immediately on the fiscal balance, public debt, monetary policy, and ultimately on internal and external macro-balance. A PAYG system may be part of the government budget or be a separate fund managed by a distinct public agency. Underlying financial contributions and claims are not affected, if properly accounted for, even in case of central government 'raids' on pension funds, but there is a difference in the degree of transparency, and therefore of accountability, associated with the formal arrangements. A FF system may be centralised but, more probably and in line with the approach's ideology, run by competing private funds.

Pension system reform

The comparison of alternative pension systems, and discussions about their reform in transition economies, have been guided – explicitly or implicitly – by the following propositions:

- that the PAYG or redistribution system, unlike the capitalisation or funded system, is necessarily a net claim on the government's budgetary resources and the ultimate cause of a rapidly mounting fiscal imbalance;
- that there are additional, clear-cut, net advantages of adopting a funded system, in terms of a higher rate of return, the development of financial markets and corporate governance, and the promotion of domestic savings;

- that there is a 'double cost' to the state of switching from a PAYG to a fully funded system, as the state still has to pay pensioners under the old PAYG regime while no longer receiving the benefit of current employee contributions which are now channelled to pension funds under the new pension regime.

These three propositions are either wrong or require heavy qualification. It will be made clear in this chapter that the move from PAYG to a fully funded system is politically rather than economically motivated. It is a function of the importance attached implicitly to individual choice and risk-taking, to the transparency of individual contributions and entitlements, and to state withdrawal from the economy. At the same time, the cost of switching from one to the other system is shown to be: (i) usually overestimated, as it consists not of an additional cost but, instead, of the surfacing of hidden costs already incurred; (ii) associated with the adverse temporal restructuring of existing pension liabilities, which still require current funding and may be made more tractable by a gradual shift; (iii) partly unnecessary, to the extent that the PAYG system can be – and should be – reformed so as to be entirely self-financed and maintained next to funded provisions, or, if it is not entirely self-financed, only that part dependant on budgetary financing needs to be converted into open and funded liabilities. Within a PAYG system reformed so as to be made fully viable, pension provisions can be individualised and made dependent on lifetime individual contributions, thus mimicking some of the advantages of the FF system.

Alternative systems: fiscal implications

PAYG schemes are widely considered to generate a pensions 'burden' (see Mortensen 1994; World Bank 1994). In most PAYG schemes current old age pensions are paid out of the contributions of those currently employed, whose future pensions in turn will be paid out of the contributions of future employees. If the scheme is considered separately from the general level of taxation and the overall budget balance then whether the scheme is 'sustainable' depends on the scheme parameters. Basically these are:

- the dependency ratio s (defined in Table 5.1) depending on demographic trends (participation rates, ageing or rejuvenating population), the unemployment rate, working and retiring ages and their trends;

- the replacement ratio r = P/W between average pension P and average wage W (depending also on their time structure, indexation provisions etc); and
- the average ratio d of individual plus employers' contributions to wages, D/W.

A current deficit occurs if d < rs, in which case total current pensions exceed total current contributions.

Any PAYG system is always viable for some level of average pension relative to average wage, regardless of the value of the dependency ratio s. It will always be viable for r = d/s, ie total current pensions equal total current contributions. Even for a falling population of employees, there is continuous replacement of employee generations and therefore – as long as the PAYG pension system is compulsory and centrally run – there is always a positive net flow of new 'depositors', which always makes possible a positive pay-out to old 'depositors', the pensioners.

A fully-funded (FF) pension scheme is one in which an individual's contributions whilst employed and the employer's contributions are used to purchase financial assets that pay the individual's pension in retirement. If it were possible to estimate with total accuracy the lifetime of the pensioner, then the fund would be perfectly exhausted at death. In fact, a rough balance between individual cumulative contributions and their cumulative yield, on the one hand, and individual cumulative pensions on the other, is achieved as an actuarial average. A FF scheme is viable if the value and yield of the accumulated fund is sufficient to pay the desired pension over an average lifetime. If the state guarantees pensioners a minimum income, then a failure to accumulate sufficient assets in a FF scheme will result in the individual being forced to accept welfare benefits from the state that will therefore be responsible for the consequences of the scheme deficit. An excess accumulation of assets typically reverts to the financial institution (or employer) providing the pension, though in some circumstances excess assets may be part of a legacy.

The PAYG system is macro-economically neutral when the scheme is balanced, ie when current contributions are equal to current pensions. A FF scheme is similarly neutral when the current sums saved to accumulate new assets (including reinvested interest and dividends on the stock of assets) are equal to the current pensions being withdrawn from stocks of assets associated with earlier schemes. The macro-economic impact of either scheme is therefore defined as the relationship between the current net flow of, on the one hand, savings and contributions (including taxes), and, on the other hand, expenditure out of pension income.

This is not to say that the two systems are equivalent in every respect. But at any given time and for given parameters (eg age structure, wage and salary growth, retirement age) individual and employer contributions in the two systems can be adjusted so as to sustain the same current level of pensions. The two systems' behaviour over time will, of course, vary according to trends in ageing, in the replacement ratio (ie the ratio between average pensions and current average wages) and in the return on pension fund assets. Pension contributions, in order to sustain macro-economic neutrality, will have to be continually adjusted. For a given level of contributions, old age pensioners would be better off in one system or another depending on the actual parameters. For instance, rejuvenation of the population improves the relative position of pensioners who are on a PAYG system compared with the unchanged position of pensioners on a fully-funded system (and vice versa when the population is ageing). Similarly, a rise in the return on pension fund assets improves the relative position of members of a FF scheme.

A fiscal burden arises, potentially in both systems, once a defined level of pension is guaranteed by the state, whether this minimum is geared to the pensioner's last level of earnings achieved, or best average over a specified period of time, or to cumulative lifetime earnings – especially if such level is indexed with respect to the consumption price index or to the current average wage in the economy. In different, but equally plausible, circumstances a fiscal burden may arise under both systems, possibly to a degree unsustainable in the long run. The burden arises in the PAYG system as soon as $d < rs$. In the funded system the burden arises as soon as the guaranteed pension is greater than that afforded by the system's parameters. The burden arises in the FF system when the stock of assets is insufficient to fund the defined level of pensions and the state accepts responsibility for meeting the difference. (An additional burden arises in the FF system from fiscal privileges granted to pension contributions, and to income earned by pension funds and capital gains made by them.)

The widespread pay-as-you-go system, which until recently prevailed in both east and west, came increasingly to burden the state budget due to i) high pension levels relative to the size and length of contributions and ii) a worsening dependency ratio between pensioners and employees (due to growing unemployment and falling population growth). A regime of fully-funded pensions would not and will not involve such a burden on the state. Though it could as soon as it became partially funded, say, if the state guaranteed a strong link between pensions and current real wages in an economy with fast growing living standards and low real interest rates. Pure systems, of course, are unusual, and mixed systems are very similar: once a minimum pension is guaranteed by the state, a funded system and a pay-as-you-go system can be equally ruinous for public finances and are virtually impossible to distinguish.

Other costs and benefits of alternative systems

A fully-funded system is usually regarded as more efficient than a pay-as-you-go system for four main reasons: i) pension funds benefit from professional management of their portfolio; ii) the funds' portfolio benefits from the high long-term return of equity investments, including capital appreciation; iii) funds enhance citizens' choice, which in turn guarantees investors' involvement and the activation of corporate governance mechanisms; iv) their introduction promotes the widening and deepening of financial markets and promotes domestic savings – the last two being advantages particularly significant in a transition economy. The Chilean example is usually quoted as a success story in all these respects.

On reflection, these expectations – as well as the significance of the Chilean case – have been exaggerated:

- professional management of competing funds involves significant transaction and administration costs, relative to a centrally-run PAYG scheme. In Chile, where a contribution equal to ten per cent of the wage is made to pension funds, the management charge is an additional two per cent of the wage.

- the real rate of return obtainable on the stock exchange depends on the starting and end points chosen. Recent Chilean success is due mostly to good timing, as the switch to a funded system was implemented at a time when the stock exchange was undervalued and poised to grow. Other reforms may turn out to be less fortunate in their timing, thus leading to pressures for continued state support. Goetzman (1997) provided estimates of return on capital for 39 markets, with histories going back as far as the 1920s. He found that the United States had the highest uninterrupted real rate of appreciation of all countries, at 4.3 per cent annually from 1921-96, but for other countries the median real appreciation rate was only 0.8 per cent. This suggests that the high return earned on US equities was the exception rather than the rule. And insofar as investment in equities confers an advantage, there are a parallel disadvantages: greater risk and volatility of performance. For instance, in 1995-96 even the Chilean stock exchange yielded a negative average rate of return, not to mention the world-wide crises of the autumns of 1987 and 1998.

- choice enhancement was certainly not a significant achievement of the Chilean model. In order to protect investors, it was stipulated that the companies running pension funds should supplement out of their own capital any performance shortfall of over two per cent from the mean rate of return of all funds. This stipulation, however, led to 'herd behaviour', with all funds choosing near-identical portfolios (Fazio and Riesco 1997). Moreover, in 1996 a concentration and consolidation process led by Chilean banks reduced the range of funds available. Such herd-like behaviour is also common among UK pension funds. An intriguing exception is provided by Czech investment funds, which offer an extraordinary variability of rates of returns, but of course at the expense of additional exposure to risk. This may lead to successful calls for a government guarantee of minimum pensions. The claimed promotion of corporate governance may require, as in Chile, significant regulation.

- reliance on pension funds for the development of financial markets and of domestic savings may also be over-played. At least some (by all accounts about one half) of the savings

> imposed by participation in pension funds instead of PAYG schemes simply goes to replace earlier voluntary savings. Clearly savings promotion is greatest the higher the share of those who under the PAYG regime had no voluntary savings at all. Moreover, additional savings may or may not be matched by additional investment; especially in a transition economy. 'Pension funds can only develop as fast as the financial infrastructure', according to an EBRD official quoted by Benoit and Vipotnik (1997). 'In view of the deterioration in income distribution during the transition period and the lack of an efficient and sound financial infrastructure for the successful operation of private pension funds, a relatively large redistributive public pension scheme may be necessary, at least for the time being, in most of these countries' (de Castello Blanco, 1998).

A funded system also requires the funds' honest administration. This demands appropriate legislation, regular publication of audited accounts, police concern with financial fraud, and so on, in order to prevent the funds from being 'tunnelled' (as has happened in Czech investment funds) or 'Maxwelled'. It is possible that a contribution to honest administration can be made by having representatives of both contributors and pensioners on the boards that control the pension funds.

Since workers typically change jobs many times in their lives, it is essential that the rights built up in a pension fund do not suffer when an employee changes jobs. It is also desirable to avoid a funded system that penalises spouses, forcing them to fall back on a residual PAYG.

In a closed economy, or the world as a whole, low values of the elasticity of savings and investment with respect to the interest rate lead to a situation in which society as a whole, unlike individuals, cannot gain command over future income by acquiring financial assets. Hence PAYG and FF systems are, macroeconomically, equivalent forms of inter-generational transfers, any supposed difference being attributable to the fallacy of composition (Eatwell 1999). This point is modified in an open economy by the fact that an economy that acquires financial assets in other countries will thereby command part of their future income (though aggregate net domestic savings and the consequential acquisition of foreign assets may derive from either taxes or private savings exceeding national investment). Income has been redistributed at one time, not through time.

An important controversy concerns the impact of different pension arrangements on real investment rates and hence on the scale of future income flows. This controversy is unresolved. Feldstein (1974) argued that PAYG schemes could reduce aggregate savings and investment. However, his work was shown to suffer from serious statistical flaws (Leimer and Lesnoy, 1982). Nor is it clear that funded schemes result in an improved allocation of savings, or better improved flows of funding to industry (Rosa, 1982; Singh, 1995).

The greatest advantage of a fully-funded system is perhaps that of adjusting pensions automatically to changing exogenous trends, such as demographic trends and above all population ageing. However, automatic adjustment mechanisms could be introduced also in a PAYG scheme, for instance making pensionable age a function of current life expectancy. If this principle were applied by gender, it would also put an end to cross-gender subsidisation, itself a product of the fact that women live longer than men but usually retire earlier.

In view of the arguments indicated above, ultimately the choice between the two systems depends on expectation about the return on financial assets, attitudes to risk, and political preferences concerning the role of the state – not on a clear-cut technical superiority of the fully funded system. Some people may prefer to accumulate pension funds which 'belong to them' and from which they derive some sense of security, rather than rely on a pension funded from taxation paid by an as-yet unborn generation[1]. Others may prefer a claim to an attractive pension from a scheme unlikely to be sustainable in the long run, to a secure fully funded but more modest claim.

PAYG pensions are defined by political rights, and consequently tend to involve some redistribution in favour of the poor, sometimes to excess, ie to a populist, non-sustainable extent. Funded schemes, conversely, tend to exacerbate the inequality of income distribution among the working population, since poorer workers typically make inadequate provision for their retirement. The argument that funded schemes 'reduce the burden of pensions' can be a euphemism for 'funded schemes cut the pensions of the poor' (Eatwell 1997); though the rich usually live longer than average, and therefore benefit from PAYG pensions more than the poor.

PAYG requires confidence in the political system (which guarantees the level of PAYG pensions) while funding requires confidence in the return on financial assets. In some countries there is more faith in the latter than in the former. When one sees how the political process in some countries (eg the UK) has cut the benefits previously promised under PAYG, this is understandable. Where there is for this reason public support for funding, this provides a good climate for developing a second tier.

Open and hidden costs of pension system reform.

There is a widespread view that the switch from a pay-as-you-go to a fully-funded system involves a costly transition period: 'The fiscal costs of undertaking such a shift may be very high' (Chand and Jaeger 1996, p2). Sometimes there is talk of 'double' cost. In fact, the cost is neither double nor is it strictly speaking a new net cost – though of course an old cost is incurred, simply on the obvious observation that initially current old age pensions cannot any longer be paid out of the current employees' contributions, which are now invested in their own pension funds.

The switch can be instantaneous. The contributions of all employees, old and new, suddenly are paid into pension funds, while the government assigns to the pension fund of each past contributor to the PAYG scheme, whether still employed or already retired, a capital lump sum corresponding to the capitalisation to date of past contributions or, for the retired, of expected pensions. On retirement, such capital lump sum can then be run down gradually while earning interest on the residual, or be used to buy an annuity. A massive additional capital expenditure that could correspond to a large share of yearly GDP, or possibly a multiple of it, is instantaneously incurred by the government at the time of a regime switch from PAYG to FF pensions.

Three observations are in order here. First the good news. The switch from a PAYG to a FF system does not involve any additional cost, but it simply brings to the surface a hidden cost already incurred and transforms it into an open one. The hidden cost is the past accumulation of liabilities towards today's old age pensioners, whose past contributions as employees had been effectively 'borrowed' in the past to pay pensions at the time. The bad news is that the new open cost, which is the payment of pension entitlements matured to date, or of their capitalisation, is a real and not just a virtual claim on the state budget, involving higher government borrowing at once, instead of being paid later. In macro-economic terms it is important that the state should not raise taxes to fund its liability, otherwise, all other things being equal, the combination of extra taxes and the new levels of private savings flowing into the funded scheme would have a deflationary impact on the economy. So long as the level and growth of GDP is maintained the switch involves no net payment by the economy as a whole.

The switch from PAYG to a FF system is very similar to another financial manoeuvre typical of the transition, namely the re-capitalisation of state enterprises and banks by the government, after the cleansing of their balance sheets through the removal of bad loans. The net wealth of the state does not change as a result of either operation but current resources have to be found to finance the repayment of hidden state debt. Conversely, as a matter of interest, a hypothetical switch from a FF to PAYG system would be equivalent to hidden state borrowing through the nationalisation of assets and liabilities of the FF system.

Second, the switch need not be instantaneous. Its burden on the state budget can be diluted over time. In a gradual switch, only the new entrants into employment move into a fully funded system, with all the others continuing to contribute and draw pensions on a PAYG system. Additional government expenditure over and above the previous level is now incurred, for the payment of the same pensions flow out of reduced contributions, but the initial imbalance is a fraction of full capitalisation and, though continuing over time, it is gradually reduced to zero on the death of the last PAYG pensioner. The switch from one system to the other is still front-loaded in terms of fiscal burden, but not as much as instant full capitalisation. The PAYG negative net present value is gradually run down, at the cost of attracting additional interest on its unpaid part, presuming that it is being run down faster than interest accumulates. The case for a gradual transition is the exactly the same as that for the rescheduling of external debt, possibly with similar requirements for 'debt relief' in the form of social recognition of the need to reduce non-sustainable pension entitlements.

An intermediate transition path from a PAYG to a FF system could also be imagined, for instance with lump sum capitalisations paid only to people not yet retired, or still employed but over a given age.

Third, the switch to a FF system need not be total, because a self-supporting PAYG segment can be left in place.

Clearly it is desirable for an unsustainable PAYG system to be reformed and made as far as possible self-supporting. But if, for the given contribution and the given replacement and support ratios, the PAYG system exhibits a deficit, this will have to be paid for out of current taxation and borrowing. The present value of these deficits over time must be matched when switching to a FF system by government contributions in cash or in government bonds earmarked for the purpose, so as to meet the liabilities accumulated under the PAYG scheme. Only any such unfunded state liability (over and above current contributions) needs, when the switch to the FF system occurs, to be capitalised and transferred to old members of the system (old age pensioners or employees) as a lump sum investible in the new pension funds.

Individualised pensions within a viable PAYG

An alternative to a partial or total switch to a FF system is the further modification of a reformed and viable PAYG so as to mimic two major properties of the FF system while still remaining within a centrally-run state system. The properties are, the link between individual pensions and individual lifetime contributions (this is a feature of an individual fully-funded pension contract but frequently not, or only in an attenuated form, of group pension funds), as well as a connection with the yield obtainable in financial markets. Systems of this kind have been adopted in Sweden and Italy, and seem popular in FSU countries.

From the moment such a reform is introduced, a part of current contributions, whether for new entrants or for a progressively rising share of all contributors, are credited to individual accounts, whether actual or 'virtual'. Their accumulation over time, augmented by a yield related to the performance of financial markets, is the basis for the calculation of individual pensions on retirement.

To some extent this arrangement is purely cosmetic, especially in its 'virtual' form of symbolically earmarking an individualised credit to individual accounts in an essentially unchanged system. The change does not involve the expected gains of promoting choice among alternative funds, developing financial markets and enhancing saving. If the contributions diverted to this system were actually locked into individual accounts, then the same problem of funding the switch from a PAYG to a FF system would still arise. In practice, this kind of change has been accompanied by parallel partial moves towards a genuine FF system. In any case, the arrangement also provides real and significant advantages, such as flexibility in allowing contributors to choose the time pattern of contributions and pensions, including retiring age, the length of the contribution period and the timing of contributions. The funds locked into individualised accounts may be used as collateral, say for funding house purchase or the cost of retraining.

PAYG as a very special Ponzi scheme, wholly or partially viable

Critics of the Pay As You Go pension system (PAYG) have likened it to a Ponzi scheme of pyramid banking, thus asserting its lack of long-term viability, its instability and 'inherently fraudulent' nature. Formally the PAYG system does indeed resemble a Ponzi scheme, but has very special, unique features that make it viable, whether in its entirety or at least on a partial scale, therefore falsifying the implications of instability or fraud.

In pyramid banking an interest rate higher than obtainable in the use of funds is paid by a bank to existing depositors out of new deposits, thus generating a negative net present value growing over time, until at some point new deposits dry up as panic sets in and the system necessarily collapses into bankruptcy. In a similar way a PAYG system can finance current pensions wholly or partly out of current employees' contributions, leaving behind a build-up of future liabilities to future old age pensioners that are not matched by a corresponding build-up of assets. Those unmatched future net liabilities have a negative present value. Just as in a Ponzi scheme the liabilities are to depositors whose new deposits have been diverted to paying interest on old deposits. But the similarity ends there. In a PAYG system seen as a Ponzi scheme new 'deposits' of pension contributions are always positive, as current employment is positive and the PAYG system is universal and compulsory, and 'withdrawals' are orderly and restricted to old age. Therefore there is always an average pension level at any time, at or below which the PAYG system, unlike Ponzi schemes of pyramid banking, is and can stay viable.

A fully-balanced Pay As You Go system, in which current pensions match exactly current contributions and there are no assets or liabilities, has zero gross assets; its net present value is negative due to future liabilities to current pensioners and employees, but as long as the system stays balanced this never comes to the surface. That net negative present value is matched, as it were, by a kind of seigniorage that the government obtains from the exclusive right to run a universal and compulsory PAYG pension system. The 'true' net present value of that PAYG system is zero, in the sense that, if the government wanted to privatise it, transferring its rights and obligations to a private institution enabled to maintain pensions at a level no greater than allowed by current contributions, there would be no need for any public compensation for the outstanding net negative present value, nor for any recurring future subsidy.

The balanced PAYG negative present value, however, surfaces when current contributions are switched to a fully-funded system. Therefore the transformation of a PAYG balanced system into a FF system is a real claim on current resources that without that transformation would never need be paid off.

An unbalanced PAYG system, paying current pensions higher than current contributions, in turn can be notionally split into a viable balanced segment and a deficit. The balanced segment can be visualised as notionally paying an average pension that exhausts current contributions; the deficit corresponds to the higher average pension paid to all old age pensioners. The considerations developed above would continue to apply only to the balanced segment of the unbalanced PAYG system.

The 'true' PAYG debt, for which the day of reckoning sooner or later will come, is only the present value of future deficits, not that of all future pensions of the current labour force. This true debt is the compensation that would have to be paid to a private institution willing to take over responsibility for continuing to run that system on a continued basis. It is clearly undesirable, non-transparent and non-sustainable to sweep those forthcoming deficits under the carpet of quasi-fiscal liabilities. It is infinitely preferable, and also transparent and sustainable, to allow such a true PAYG debt to surface at once, endowing the PAYG system (through the Fund, or the Agency running it) with government bonds matching in amounts and maturities future uncovered pension liabilities, and to keep meeting any possible yearly increase in such a true PAYG debt out of the government budget. If a FF system was deemed to have other advantages (besides sustainability), a conversion of the true PAYG debt into a FF system would yield those advantages at no extra cost, other than that of funding that part of government debt which FF pension funds would not retain in their portfolios. In order to reduce this extra cost, the conversion of the true PAYG debt could be done gradually over time. This seems a superior alternative to the conversion of the entire PAYG system to FF, which would bring about the surfacing and additional current cost of the entire negative net present value of the PAYG system. In either case, the state's net wealth is unaffected by the operation, but the conversion of the entire PAYG system has an unnecessary current cost, for the sole purpose of beautifying the pension system.

The status of pension reform in transition economies

A summary of progress to date in pension reform in transition economies is provided in Table 5.4.

Hungary was the first country to introduce a mandatory funded pillar replacing part of the PAYG system, in a move similar to Argentina's experience (Rutkowski, 1998). From 1 July 1998 all those entering employment for the first time have been legally obliged to pay 25 per cent of their pension contributions, which amount to 30 per

Table 5.4 Pension reform progress in transition economies (end 1997)
P=Preparation, A=Approved, L=Legislated

	Comprehensive reform programme			*Second pillar introduction*			*Major first pillar reform*			*Major third pillar reform*		
	P	*A*	*L*	*P*	*A*	*L*	*P*	*A*	*L*	*P*	*A*	*L*
Hungary		x	x		x	x		x	x		x	x
Latvia		x			x			x				
Poland		x			x	x		x			x	x
Kazakhstan		x	x		x	x		x	x			
Czech Republic	x			x			x				x	x
Slovenia	x			x			x			x		
Russia	x			x			x					
Croatia	x			x			x					
FYROM	x			x			x					
Bulgaria	x			x			x			x		
Romania	x			x			x			x		
Armenia							x					
Lithuania									x	x		
Slovakia							x				x	

Source: Rutkowski (1998)

cent of the wage, into private pension schemes, with the rest going into the public pension plan. Those already employed had the option of continuing with the present wholly state system for another 15 years. The World Bank provided a $150 million nine-year loan, with a three-year grace period, to assist this reform (*Financial Times* 30 January 1998). The Slovenian approach is similar to the Hungarian.

Kazakhstan aims at replicating the Chilean pension system in one go, with mandatory, privately managed, funded pension schemes absorbing 10 per cent of payroll (de Castello Blanco 1998). Temporarily, the lack of a developed financial market is forcing the accumulation of contributions in government bonds, with a view to subsequent redeployment.

Croatia has plans for a modest reform, with a relatively small UK-style flat-rate benefit, a funded component at 5-7 per cent of payroll and no emphasis on voluntary pension provisions. There is some discussion of mandatory funded pillars in Macedonia and Romania (Rutkowski 1998).

Poland has moved towards a three-pillar system. Under the new pension insurance system applicable from 1 January 1999 all insured have individual accounts, containing information on cumulated credits and resulting pension entitlement. Older participants retain the option to stay with the old system (at a cost). A Demographic Reserve Fund, FRD, collects any current surplus to cover any deficit derived from adverse demographic trends. The first pillar pension is obtained by dividing the individual cumulated balance by the average (regardless of gender) life expectancy on retirement, prospectively fixed at 62 for both genders (an alternative of 62 for women and 65 for men is still under discussion). Pensions being indexed to prices, a zero real rate of return is involved. The second pillar involves mandatory participation in freely chosen privately managed pension funds.

The Polish approach has the additional attractive feature (adopted also by Kazakhstan) of utilising residual state assets, already slated for privatisation but still in Treasury hands, as a source of funding the partial move from PAYG to a FF segment in the new mixed system. The realisation that the old PAYG system involves a submerged public debt that now surfaces, although its impact can be greatly reduced following the above recommendations, should discourage any suggestion of free (or heavily subsidised) voucher privatisation as irresponsible populism.

Latvia has chosen a gradual move towards a balanced mix between PAYG and funded systems, resembling the Swiss model (de Castello Blanco, 1998).

The Russian government's draft plan for pension reform was approved on 18 December 1997. It proposed that future pensions should be funded from three components: a basic contribution from the state, mandatory contributions paid by the worker into the national Pension Fund, and voluntary contributions by the worker to private pension funds (see *Bank of Finland, Russian and Baltic Economies – Weekly Review* 9 January 1998). Mandatory occupational pensions are to replace the special favours enjoyed by particular employee groups and sectors. Belarus has adopted, by virtue of obligations resulting from its Economic and Social Union with Russia, a similar approach.

It is not clear whether the Russian/Belarussian pension reform package involves a partial switch to a FF system, in which case the cost of switching, estimated around $5 billion, has been unduly neglected, or is a purely 'virtual' Swedish-Italian type of change, in which case the very slow gradualism in its introduction is unnecessary. It is significant that opposition to the Russian plans should have come not only from the left but also from World Bank officials 'who say they opposed the idea because they feared that Russia was moving too hastily to a fully-privatised system, which could falter or even collapse' (*New York Times* 15 March 1998).

A major difficulty is that the Russian/Belarussian reform is designed against a background of a still non-viable PAYG system, as confirmed in Russia by the continued existence of pension arrears and in Belarus by state enterprise inability to pay pension contributions. It is therefore devoid of credibility. Another major difficulty for Russian reform is the high risk and extreme uncertainty concerning the real return on financial assets. The default by the government on its own debts in August 1998 was a striking example of this. Under these circumstances a funded scheme is not viable, as the World Bank specialists had already pointed out.

The Czech Republic, Lithuania and Albania moved early, but undertook only relatively modest reform of their PAYG schemes, with only a 35-40 per cent target replacement ratio between average pension and wage, and a mixed formula for determining pension entitlement based on both years of service and earnings. Voluntary private schemes are also contemplated.

In the poorer countries such as Kyrgyzstan and Mongolia, and in countries like Ukraine, where the transformation has stagnated or regressed, the only reform envisaged is that towards a more sustainable PAYG system (Rutkowski 1998).

Policy recommendations

Clearly there is no 'ideal model' for pension reform. Against the checkered background of pension reform attempts in different transition economies, however, the considerations and arguments developed earlier indicate the following course as being, by far, the best approach for a country that has inherited a non-sustainable PAYG system:

- scaling down generosity towards pensioners in order to bring the system closer to sustainable levels, through reduced benefits (including loss of indexation, or indexation to prices rather than wages) and/or increased contributions and/or longer working life (also for the sake of inter-generational fairness, subject to social consensus);

- if there is a positive political assessment of the net advantages of a FF system, its introduction through the transformation of that part of the old PAYG system which is not financed by contributions and has to be covered anyway by government subsidies, into individual accounts within the new funded pension scheme (the so-called second pillar);
- the promotion of a third pillar of voluntary private savings, preferably with some tax-privileges in order to partially compensate for any initial scaling down of pension provisions with respect to the former PAYG;
- possibly, if the advantages of a funded system are deemed overwhelming, its gradual extension on a partial basis (in the sense of coexisting with a reformed PAYG) for the newly employed, if and when the cost of switching from PAYG to a funded system can be borne by the government budget.

The end result of these recommendations is a potential three-pillar system, apparently similar to that advocated by the World Bank (1994), or being implemented in most transition economies. The third pillar of voluntary savings is, of course, always actually or potentially present whatever the pension system and its parameters, and cannot be considered as a distinctive feature of any reform. There are, however, very substantial differences between the recommendations listed above and those of the World Bank (1994) in that here:

- the first pillar is strengthened and maintained in its own right and with its own function, rather than as an indestructible monument to existing rigidities, inflexibilities and soft budgets;
- a FF component is introduced not as a technically superior solution but as a primarily political, though entirely respectable, solution;
- the switch from PAYG to FF is not instantaneous and total, which would unnecessarily add to current government borrowing requirements, with adverse impact on inflation and growth.

The above recommendations are also different from the rationale of the Polish three-pillar system, which rests on the stated ground of 'Security through Diversity'. Diversification is always an added attraction of the three-pillar system, but the underlying case for that system, for the reasons and in the proportions specified here, is much stronger.

Endnotes

1. The sense of security may of course, be false, since the future pension depends on the real value of the returns to the fund. Ultimately this depends on the real rate of growth, as does the tax base of a PAYG pension scheme.

6. Income transfers and anti-poverty policy

Equality and growth

This chapter addresses two questions that are clearly interrelated, yet are at the same time distinct: inequality and poverty. Even substantial economic growth, which in some transition countries is still only a dream for the future, will not eliminate these problems. In the policy debate, poverty has made all the running. It is always the more urgent question. However, a good society will also be concerned about the consequences of excessive inequality. As was demonstrated by the wealth of argument and empirical evidence assembled in their path-breaking book by Andrew Glyn and David Miliband (1994), greater equality is associated with lower levels of crime, higher life expectancy and a greater level of well-being as measured by a range of social indicators.

With respect to the distribution of income the countries of central and eastern Europe are very sharply distinguished (see Table 1.1 in Chapter One). Amongst those further west, where the transition shock to output and income was (relatively) small, the expected widening in income distribution was more modest. In the European successor states of the former Soviet Union, there have been far greater income and output shocks and very large increases in measures of income inequality. Bulgaria and Romania occupy an expected intermediate position (Flemming, 1998).

It is often presumed that a widening in income differentials is desirable. The relatively limited increase in standard measures of inequality in the countries with the most favourable experience may have been inevitable. The increases have generally brought inequality in the Central European states into line with inequality in EU member states. Certainly the prohibition of most legal entrepreneurial activity in the old system suppressed part of the income range, while the privileges of the nomenklatura were often not properly imputed. At the lower end of the scale totalitarian mechanisms kept in check a substantial contingent who will tend to be marginalised in less repressive societies: life-long alcoholics and recidivists, for example.

There is, however, no reason in economic theory nor in historical experience to suggest that the larger increases in standard measures of inequality in some countries are 'natural', necessary or desirable. In the Russian Federation inequality as measured either by the Gini coefficient or by the ratio of income shares of the top and bottom 20 per cent, is approaching levels close to that of Latin America. Whilst the income levels in Latin America and many central and eastern European countries are comparable, structurally and socially they have had very different trajectories of development. The extremely high levels of inequality in much of Latin America are the legacy of a large uneducated work force, a dual economy with a small modern sector, large and relatively unintegrated backward regions, and, of course, the legacy of colonialism and slavery (Iglesias, 1998).

Acceptance that it is 'inevitable' that much of the former Soviet Union will come to resemble the worst features of Latin America is in part a mistaken legacy of the impact of the 'Kuznets hypothesis', which has strongly influenced much thinking on economic growth and development. This hypothesis suggests that the road to greater prosperity must pass first through greater inequality. Virtually all the recent evidence suggests otherwise (Tanzi and Chu, 1998). Dani Rodrik, as a discussant, summed up the results of an IMF conference on the subject in the following terms: 'The Kuznets curve is a fiction. There is no systematic relationship between income levels and inequality'. Nor, he stressed, do adjustment policies have to be inherently detrimental to equity.

With the rejection of the Kuznets Hypothesis there is no new conventional wisdom on this central economic question of the interconnections between equality and growth, 'the jury is still out'. There is, however, an emerging consensus that, at least: 'The view that there necessarily is a trade-off between efficiency and equity, or with the developing countries, between growth and equity, has been discredited' (Stiglitz, in Tanzi and Chu, 1998). An increasing number of studies do suggest that initial equity is good for growth, though this is still a matter of controversy.

Is income distribution really amenable to change? Here too the pessimistic view appears to be unfounded. In most industrialised countries income differentials before taxes and transfers widened in the 1980s. It is not true, however, that all societies have experienced growing inequality in the 1980s and 1990s. In Australia, Canada, France, the Federal Republic of Germany and Sweden widening pre-tax differentials were effectively countered by active redistribution measures. In Britain and the United States the trends in transfers and taxes went the other way (Gottschalk, 1993; Brandolini and Rossi, in Tanzi and Chu, 1998).

There is, of course, the reasonable fear that excessive public spending to promote egalitarian measures in central and eastern Europeans will hinder the development of small and medium sized firms and will 'crowd out' the private investment which is critical as the engine of economic modernisation and growth and the means of achieving the levels of living in the European Union. This is a legitimate concern. But here too, the most recent discussion calls sharply into question the idea that reduced social expenditure and diminished public investment is necessary for growth.

Lindert (1996) presents a powerful and accessible empirically grounded argument that social spending does not deter growth. He points out the elementary flaws in the econometric work of those who sought to limit social spending everywhere (for example, Barro and Lee, 1994) and who shaped the conventional wisdom on this topic for most of the 1990s. Relying on OECD-economy outliers like Japan or 'putting dictators like Mobutu or Kaunda or Marcos into your statistical sample will of course turn up large costs of government' (p21). Lindert's important conclusion, for transition Europe, is an optimistic one. Electoral democracy is important for eventually setting government on the path towards growth and efficiency, as well as social justice.

Land (re)distribution as an anti-poverty measure

A very common policy measure implemented throughout the transformation countries has been a widespread (re)distribution of land. That has formed part of a comprehensive land reform programme. In the rural areas of many countries, from Albania to Georgia, the newly distributed plots of land are a major source of real income for the population. This is particularly so in the FSU countries. According to official statistics, in 1996 in Russia the small household plots of land (this excludes the larger and more market-oriented family farms) produced 90 per cent of all potatoes, 77 per cent of all vegetables, 52 per cent of meat, 45 per cent of milk and 31 per cent of eggs. Indeed, according to Russian official statistics, in 1996 43 per cent of all the food consumed by Russian households came from these small plots. If this is true, it is remarkable evidence of the decreasing importance of the division of labour in Russia and of the general primitivisation of its economy (Hedlund & Sundstrom, 1996).

An interesting and important question is whether this land reform programme has been an effective anti-poverty programme. Indeed, does the widespread phenomenon (especially in the FSU) of urban households who devote a large amount of time to cultivating their plot of land, obviate the need for a more modern (employment and cash-benefit oriented) anti-poverty programme? Research on the income distribution effects of these plots in Russia based on sample surveys undertaken by independent academic researchers shows that most of the food produced goes to the middle and upper income strata and that the poorest part of the population benefits very little from such plots (Seeth *et al*, 1998; Clarke, 1998). This suggests that in Russia the widespread distribution of small plots of land was an effective policy to raise average real incomes, especially of rural inhabitants, but is not a substitute for an effective anti-poverty programme. However, official Russian statistics (which are derived from the not very reliable official national household budget survey) indicate that in 1996 the poorest decile of the urban population provided the largest proportion of their food (29 per cent) by self-production (Rimashevskaya *et al*, 1998, pp197-8). Even these statistics, however, showed that for the urban very poor, the ten per cent of the urban population with the lowest incomes, the overwhelming proportion of their food (71 per cent) had to be purchased with money. The official consumption statistics also indicated that in 1996 the poorest ten per cent of the urban population consumed only about 72 per cent of the official poverty line level of energy, measured in calories, and 54 per cent of the official poverty line level of protein. The position of the second decile was not much better, 79 per cent and 60 per cent respectively. These figures indicate the existence of a serious malnutrition problem that may be alleviated, but is not eliminated by the cultivation of small plots of land. Nor, of course, does the existence of plots meet the non-food requirements of the poor.

The Roma

One group that lives in poverty throughout central and eastern Europe (and frequently also in western Europe) are the Roma. They tend to have high unemployment, low incomes, poor housing and poor education. It seems that in some respects their economic position has been worsened by transition. Under the old regime they often had jobs in industrial enterprises that have now restructured or closed down completely. In market economies the need for unskilled workers is much less than under state socialism. They were the victims of genocide under the Nazis, and have been subject to extensive violence and discrimination in recent years.

In 1992-93 the employment rate among Hungarian Roma women was only 17 per cent, and the male Roma employment rate only twice that, whereas even the now much lower employment rate for the non-Roma had only dropped from 87 per cent to 63 per cent (as a result of early retirement as well as unemployment). This dramatic difference in employment rates in 1992-93 may be contrasted with the situation in 1971, when there was no significant difference in employment between the two groups.

Recently considerable attention has been devoted to the plight of this group by organisations such as the Council of Europe and the OSCE. The well-known speculator and philanthropist George Soros has donated money to Roma causes. Some governments, such as that of Hungary, have begun to formulate enlightened policies on this issue. Nevertheless, the provision of education and housing for the Roma, so that they can obtain jobs and earn reasonable incomes, everywhere lags behind what is needed to achieve social inclusion within a reasonable period. One of the few positive developments with respect to the Roma in recent years is that they have begun to establish their own organisations and hence have acquired a greater political presence. From being an object of social policy they are slowly developing into an interest group in a pluralist society. However, the problem of poverty among them is bound to persist as long as their educational level remains low and they are unqualified for well-paid work. Obvious relevant public policies are, positive discrimination in the allocation of jobs and public contracts (in 1998 the Czech Minister without portfolio Mlynar who was responsible for Roma affairs suggested that firms owned by or employing Roma should receive about five per cent of all government orders), ensuring that Roma have the same rights in the fields of transfer payments and medical care as the rest of the population, and ensuring that Roma children attend school.

Widening the tax base

Under conditions of 'building capitalism' and privatisation, it is clearly undesirable to have marginal tax rates on the income of business people or on profits that discourage work or investment. On the other hand, it is extremely undesirable to have large informal sectors that pay no taxes and large-scale capital flight that also escapes taxes. Under these conditions widening the tax base so as to generate revenue for social programmes is of great importance. Reducing the relative size of the informal sector is something that takes time and requires that the state create acceptable rules of the game for businesses and business people. Similarly, reducing capital flight requires the creation of a stable and attractive political and economic framework. This also takes time. It might however be accelerated by cooperation between the national authorities and those western countries where most of the exported money is deposited, invested or laundered. Unfortunately, this will probably have to wait for a time when some of the leaders of the transition countries concerned are not themselves involved in capital flight. One way of widening the tax base that does not require such a long time horizon is registering and taxing real estate and durable consumer goods (in particular cars and boats). In this connection the plan of the former Polish Finance Minister Kołodko to introduce a tax on the value of land to finance local authorities seems very sensible, although it might be administratively demanding for some countries (it required valuing all land in the country). Unfortunately, Kołodko's plan failed to surmount political and technical objections, and was not implemented.

Safety net vs income replacement

There are two different philosophies of income transfers to meet the risks of unemployment, illness, or disability. There is the safety net philosophy, supported by the IMF and World Bank, which is concerned with creating and maintaining institutions which enable those hit by these calamities to receive a temporary minimal income from the state. This has the advantages of providing some help to those who experience these calamities, at a minimal fiscal cost, and providing incentives to return to the labour market as soon as possible. The other philosophy is the social insurance philosophy, which provides income related benefits in exchange for social insurance contributions paid by employees and employers. It is this latter philosophy that is dominant in the social market economies of the EU.

In general, the transition countries initially tried to introduce social insurance schemes. But as unemployment increased, fiscal problems worsened, the burden of social security contributions grew, and perceptions shifted from the unemployed as victims to the unemployed as shirkers, the tendency was to move in the direction of the safety net philosophy. Today, as Elster *et al* (1998 p215) have observed, 'all schemes now operate *de facto* as *flat-rate systems*' and 'all schemes provide only modest income support for the unemployed'. This means that many of those in receipt of these benefits will experience significant income loss, may experience poverty, and are very likely to do so once the temporary benefits have expired. Furthermore, one of the alleged benefits of the safety net philosophy, a quick return to work by the unemployed, has failed to materialise in many transformation countries.

The seductive appeal of means testing

Empirical evidence on levels of poverty in central and eastern Europe presents a strikingly diverse picture, made all the more complicated because poverty has no single definition. In the Human Development Report for the Czech Republic (1996) it is stated that 'According to the methods used in countries of the European Union, poverty in the country is lower than in most West European countries', although 35-40 per cent of the Czech population consider themselves poor. For Moldova the World Bank's uniform poverty line, $4 a day, was not achieved by an estimated 65 per cent of the population in 1993 (World Bank, 1997). For the Russian Federation, containing half the region's poor by any count, the Bank's parallel estimate was 43 per cent of the population.

Despite the diversity of evidence and experience and the rate of change in legislation and practice on income transfers, some key generalisations may be made about the direction of policy. Central and eastern European countries are trying to repeat, indeed often exceed, the western European approach by shifting from universal benefits to means testing of social benefits. This is being done in a fraction of the time taken for such developments in western Europe, with no attention given to the critical negative lessons of western experience (as outlined, for example, in OECD, 1997).

The new formula is 'targeting the most vulnerable' (World Bank, 1996). In practice, this means one type of targeting only: means-testing, whether directly or by proxy variables. Child benefits, for example, which had been universal are now widely means-tested, and means-tested housing benefit is being introduced as rents rise.

The major problem with the provision of a large part of social benefits via means testing, is that this will greatly reinforce the 'poverty trap' (the presence of very high marginal effective tax rates on the incomes and work efforts of the poor). As a household manages to increase its pre-transfer income, benefits are withdrawn and taxes have to be paid. A major OECD (1997) report recently drew the international lessons of this, beginning trenchantly: 'If work does not pay, people will be reluctant to work'.

The increased emphasis on means testing in western Europe (the number in receipt of such benefits tripled in western European countries from 1980 to 1992) was as logical at the time to western policy-makers as is now the case in the eastern half of the continent. The shift to means testing was a reaction to greater fiscal pressures, the desire to cut taxes, worries about slow growth and the impact of taxation on international competitiveness, increased demands on the public purse as the result of increased long-term unemployment, and a desire not to waste money on those not truly needy. All led in the same direction. As a result, the OECD has found present-day rates of marginal effective taxation in France for one-earner couples of 78 per cent, for those whose earnings fall in the broad range from 57 per cent to 91 per cent of average production workers' earnings. In Ireland the marginal rate was 105.5 per cent for those receiving 62-76 per cent of average earnings! In Sweden the highest effective tax rate was 'only' 72 per cent in 1994 and was paid at a much higher point in the income distribution, 147-160 per cent of average production workers' wages (OECD, 1997). These measures of marginal tax rates, noted the OECD, actually underestimate the problem.

The disadvantage of means-tested benefits is not confined to the creation of a poverty trap. As explained in Chapter 1, there are three more major problems: targeting creates a clear incentive for fraud, targeting is very expensive to administer, and targeting normally achieves less, sometimes much less, than 100 per cent take-up (often as a result of stigmatisation). The World Bank has commented on the trend toward targeting that, 'Such changes are driven more by a need to contain expenditures rather than by a desire to help the poor. Thus the focus is often on keeping individuals off the benefit system rather than ensuring full coverage of the target population' (World Bank, 1997).

The costs of identifying the target population, minimising fraud, and distributing a targeted benefit can be extremely high and may well exceed the deadweight losses implicit in un-targeted distribution. In particular, in economies with high shares of the informal sector in economic activity and personal incomes (and this is the case in many transition economies), trying to assess 'income' is an administrative nightmare and often completely impossible.

In Chapter 1 it was argued that targeted benefits therefore tend to be most efficient when: (a) targeting is not based on a means test; (b) the benefit is relatively small compared to potential income; (c) the targeted population is easy to identify, children, for example, or the blind; (d) the targeted population is a relatively small proportion of the population as a whole. Where these conditions do not apply, the transactions cost of supplying targeted benefits may well be very high indeed and instead of saving money, targeted benefits may result in substantial waste.

The problem of the poverty trap has increased in western Europe. No magic formula has been found to avoid these problems, only a set of better designs to reduce their impact. No single measure is adequate to the task. Anti-poverty policy has to be shifted from the short-termism that tends to keep the poor poor and unemployed, to a longer-term policy of assisting the poor to find work that pays a decent wage. This goal is to increase pre-transfer incomes and to reduce the taxes and social security contributions which fall on low paid workers, through easing labour market entry, not discouraging working spouses, reducing net tax and social security contributions by low earners, allowing part-time work to be viable for lone parents, and, more generally, allowing significant reward from increased effort. The policy problem is that, especially in the short term, this approach appears to be more expensive than the alternative. Lower benefits, perhaps leaving many truly poor, would, after all, reduce the disincentive problem!

The most satisfactory solution would be a high floor for everyone, and a long income interval or 'taper' in which a household earning more can keep at least 50 per cent of the fruits of its efforts. After all, it is widely believed that at the higher end of the income scale, this is the highest marginal tax rate that should be considered! Unfortunately, this optimal approach is very expensive. That is why it is probably necessary to turn to second-best solutions which involve a mix of universal benefits, together with those targeted benefits which most nearly satisfy conditions (a)-(d) above.

Targeting benefits is clearly attractive to policy-makers operating under tight fiscal constraints. But, as well as being 'economical', it is also argued that targeting will identify the truly needy. But, in fact, many poor slip through the large holes of the safety net (Standing, 1996). The argument that the vulnerable can be helped by deepening means-tested targeting should be evaluated in light of the fact that in Russia an estimated one-fifth of the poor and one-third of the very poorest fail to receive any social transfers whatsoever. This is compelling evidence of programme design errors. Indeed, there is a sleight of hand in the suggestion that means testing will help. All international experience suggests the opposite. The stigma, red tape and, especially in central and eastern European countries, the distrust of government and the pervasive grey economy, mean that even more people will be missed.

In the longer run the negative impact of means-tested benefits on incentives to work will grow stronger. This is what has happened in western Europe and the United States. Those with few ties to the labour force, and much time on their hands, will be drawn to areas with cheaper housing, but poor transport and services. Whether this is the British inner city, the French suburb, or the future undesirable district of crumbling Soviet-built blocks without amenities, the social segregation this represents is not simply inequitable: it is costly to all. It grows more costly every year.

The feminisation of poverty

A second key policy conclusion is that means-testing social benefits, and the consequential deepening of the various 'traps' of poverty, will have a particularly negative impact on the further 'feminisation of poverty' in central and eastern Europe. The work disincentive hits western single-parent families particularly sharply. The welfare of the single-parent family will surely be one of the key items on the agenda in the coming years, both for society in general and for women in particular. The benefit systems that are being established in the east offer a particular disincentive to part-time work. Western authorities have learnt that increased childcare costs and decreased childcare facilities diminish the opportunity for women to participate in education, training and work. Policies in the east are repeating western mistakes.

The problems of affordability and fiscal constraint are, of course, very real. Indeed, services in central and eastern Europe must reduce the luxurious staffing standards that prevailed when kindergarten teachers and even skilled doctors were very cheap. The cost, however, of excluding a substantial section of the population from the labour market can be very great in the long run.

The present trend also discourages the working wife. Given the 'modern' divorce rates of the region, this is also a recipe for many future difficulties. The changes in benefits may leave many women with only 'associate' status through their husbands. Social policies that are not woman-friendly are being introduced, not with particular malicious design, but in the absence of any effective voice for women.

A good example of the harmful effects of means testing concerns child benefits. Paradoxically, it was in the first, most difficult transition years that some countries maintained more universal child benefits or family assistance. Where the payments were generous (and not quickly eroded by very high inflation), this system had a remarkable impact on extreme poverty. For example, 64 per cent of households received such a benefit in Slovakia in 1993. As a result, the poverty rate (using the social minimum pension as the poverty line), went from 43.8 per cent of all families with one non-working spouse to 4.4 per cent (OECD, 1996). The OECD accurately described the change to means-testing in 1994: 'The redistributive aspects of these benefits has been improved as a result of increased targeting...although this is also likely to imply very high effective marginal tax rates for spouses who have low earnings' prospects' (OECD, 1996). Indeed, in the new Slovak system a couple with two young children could receive more than average earnings if they did not work! The OECD's comment on this was: 'In ensuring an adequate, albeit basic, living standard for larger families, this system also risks leading to lower participation and increased dependency on social support among some recipients'.

Benefits in kind

An important anti-poverty measure in many countries has been rent controls and subsidised utility prices. These provide a large benefit in kind for tenants, many of whom may be initially poor, or may become poor in the course of the transformation. For example, the Czech Republic, despite Klaus's verbal support for a 'market economy without adjectives', has maintained a fairly strong system of rent control. As is well known from western experience, rent control can have adverse effects on the maintenance of the housing stock, new construction, and labour mobility. Furthermore, its distributive effect in the transition countries is a matter of debate (see Chapter 4). In addition, low, or no, payments for utilities, may cause non-payment of the wages of workers in the utility sectors.

Nevertheless, as a temporary measure under conditions of rapid social change and extreme fiscal stringency, rent controls and subsidised utility prices are not without their merits. Not only may such measures contribute to alleviating poverty, they may also function as an internationally accepted export subsidy (since wages may be lower than they would have otherwise have been). To raise rents (and utility payments) to market levels in the absence of increased transfer payments will mean that many people (for example, pensioners) will have to be evicted from their homes. To raise rents to market levels and provide housing allowances to cushion the effect on the poor, may well turn out to be administratively difficult and a major fiscal burden. Of course in the long run this second-best solution should be phased out in favour of the optimal, though potentially expensive, policy of a high income floor for everyone and a long 'taper' in which a household earning more can keep at least 50 per cent of the fruits of its efforts.

Another important benefit in kind is food. Many countries have programmes to provide free or heavily subsidised vitamin supplements and high quality nutrition for pregnant women, babies, and nursery and primary school children. Such programmes are relatively cheap and are extremely efficient, since the improved nutrition may bring benefits throughout the life of the person concerned. The need for such programmes is, unfortunately, very pressing in the transition countries, since a number of surveys have suggested the existence of serious malnutrition problems among a section of the population. According to the UNDP (1999 p22-23) ten per cent of Polish children are permanently malnourished, and in Russia between 1992 and 1994 the prevalence of stunting among children under two increased from 9.4 per cent to 15.2 per cent. In the UK, a significant initial result of the Labour Party joining the government in May 1940 was that from the autumn of that year UK primary schools provided their children with free milk. This may be a relevant example for social democratic parties in transition countries.

Special needs groups

Even if countries are successful in continuing (or attaining) substantial economic growth, increasing employment and reducing unemployment, there will still remain groups with special needs, such as the disabled. Such groups can be helped by national transfer payment benefit programmes, benefits in kind (for example, the provision of free or subsidised Braille literature or guide dogs, or the modification of housing), employment quotas, sheltered employment, and wheelchair-friendly buildings. Experience in the Netherlands shows, however, that relatively generous transfer payments to the disabled, combined with their use by employers as a 'civilised' way of getting rid of older employees, can greatly increase the number of 'disabled' and generate a substantial burden of non-activity on the working population. The number of 'disabled' is not independent of the social attitude to 'disability'. People adapt their behaviour in response to the possibilities created by well-meaning social programmes.

In addition, international experience suggests that strong local government, together with non-governmental organisations, can be very effective in developing programmes to meet the special needs of such groups.

Conclusions

- Anti-poverty and inequality-reducing programmes are not purely an 'economic burden'. International experience shows that greater equality is positively associated with a wide range of social indicators and has discredited the 'Kuznets hypothesis'.

- Land (re)distribution has been an effective policy to raise average real incomes, particularly of rural inhabitants, in many countries It is not, however, a good substitute for a more modern (employment and cash-benefit oriented) anti-poverty programme.
- To raise revenue to finance social programmes it is important to widen the tax base. This involves a variety of measures aimed at reducing the relative size of the informal sector, reducing capital flight, and increasing taxes on real estate and consumer durables, for example, cars and boats.
- The inefficiencies of means-tested benefits suggest that an effective policy option is to restore the emphasis on universal child benefit/family allowances. Universal child benefits were introduced in western Europe when per capita GDP was not higher than that in eastern Europe now. The question is not affordability, but willingness to pay. The fact that children have been hardest hit by the transition is an unacceptable long-term risk. Moreover, the very low transactions costs of universal child benefit, make this one of the most cost effective ways of tackling poverty.
- Economies in child benefit are possible. Benefit could start at the second child. Or benefits could be integrated into the tax and benefit structure. The social solidarity and investment in human capital of child benefit is affordable. Means testing child benefits is a mistake.
- Where there are means-tested benefits, they should be designed so that each member of the household has an incentive to work. Employment-conditional benefits for families can be used to increase the in-work incomes of families.
- In countries with significant Roma populations, protecting them from persecution and co-operating with Roma organisations to raise their incomes and provide them with jobs, medical care, education and transfer payments (where appropriate), must form part of effective anti-poverty programmes.
- A striking proportion of poverty in the region is made up of working poor. In the longer term, restructuring, investment and

economic growth must be the main answer to this. If, however, a substantial portion of the population is long detached from the labour force, this 'long term' will come far too late for them, and will also provide the wrong environment for their children.

- Benefits in kind (housing, nutrition) can play a useful role in combating poverty. Temporary rent controls, and food for vulnerable groups, can play a useful role in social policy.
- All social benefit changes should be transparent, and widely discussed. The specific impact on women of each measure should be considered automatically.
- Even when policy is successful in creating employment, there will, nonetheless, remain the problem of specific groups of the population, for example the disabled. Although national programmes to meet their special needs are important, experience indicates that strong local government, together with non-governmental organisations, can be very effective in developing programmes to meet the special needs of such groups.

7. A summing up

The conclusions of the individual chapters above contain a number of detailed policy proposals, which are summarised below. Whilst these proposals cover a diverse range of issues, they are linked by a single theme, the need to comprehensively evaluate the contribution of public policy measures to the attainment of social and economic goals. Comprehensive evaluation is necessary, since the immediate impact of social policies can have unintended consequences: a badly-designed policy to redistribute income may result in lower growth and lower long-term incomes; the introduction of means-tested benefits to reduce waste may result in even greater wasteful expenditures on the complex administration and controls needed to identify 'deserving' recipients.

The welfare state should be part of an efficient economic policy. Amongst other goals, it should encourage employment and growth, develop skills and sustain technical innovation, promote social cohesion and opportunities for all, and provide a foundation of personal security upon which every person can realise their full potential.

In the economic transformation of central and eastern Europe, social policy and the welfare state have further, yet more important, roles. First, the process of transformation is inevitably painful, particularly in an era in which the entire world economy is undergoing rapid change. It is vital that everyone in society should have a stake in the success of the transformation. Secondly, the countries of central and eastern Europe are undertaking a unique task in building new societies from a failed inheritance. Decisions made now will inevitably shape their societies in the future. The commitments to social solidarity, to an inclusive society, and to economic opportunity for all, made today, will not only enhance the efficiency of the process of transformation, but also contribute to the development of successful states and a successful Europe.

Summary

Social Policy

In a number of important respects (inequality, poverty, participation, unemployment) the transition in central and eastern Europe has led to a sharp decline in welfare. This decline varies between countries. Russia and Ukraine appear to have been the most badly affected. Other countries, such as Romania, Bulgaria, and Lithuania have also experienced significant welfare declines. Nonetheless, welfare policy has evolved substantially since the beginning of the transition. Some benefits for which the need has increased the most (eg unemployment benefits) have often become the most inadequate. A major role has been played by transition-specific problems such as the need to rebuild the public sector so that it is capable of delivering efficient and high quality programmes. Of course, in the context of the economic difficulties encountered in transition, social programmes are subject to financial, administrative and economic constraints. For whilst welfare programmes normally reduce inequality and poverty in the short run, their effect on efficiency may be positive or negative, depending on the circumstances. Welfare programmes may reduce efficiency ('welfare without work', the poverty trap) or increase it (by raising participation, improving the health and increasing the skills of the population).

The contemporary challenge in all Europe is to design social programmes which not only have a positive effect on income distribution and poverty reduction but which also raise efficiency. The welfare state can increase efficiency because it provides goods and services (such as social insurance) that the market does not provide, or provides at high cost (eg pensions) or which for technical reasons (such as uncertainty, information problems, and their public goods character) the market cannot provide efficiently.

The challenge for the transition countries is to design a welfare state which provides these goods and services subject to the severe constraints under which they operate and to the potential inefficiency of the bureaucratic allocation of resources. Transfer payments and publicly provided goods and services should be regularly audited for value for money and correspondence to the preferences of the population.

Employment

The best social policy is full employment. However, the kind of full employment which existed under the old regime, and which exists in Ukraine today, is incompatible with the goals of the transformation process. The challenge to policy-makers is to recognise their responsibility to devise policies that generate 'real jobs' on a sufficient scale to combine low unemployment with transformation. This necessitates continuation of the transformation process and implementation of job creation both on the demand and on the supply sides. On the supply side, education and training, active labour market policies (such as counselling, (re)training and public works), and attention to social cohesion, are particularly important. On the demand side, the attainment and continuation of economic growth is of fundamental importance for job creation and for economic modernisation. Both aspects of employment policy must today be formulated and implemented in an environment characterised both by regional and global integration.

Health

Health care should be a public service. Insurance based health systems are very inefficient.

The fundamental goal should be the creation of a true public health system, in which medical care and medical professionals are a co-operative part. In place of the idea of omniscient medicine, the emphasis must be on examination of results, on broader co-operation within medicine, and between medicine, community and social care. Evidence, research and the critical absorption of new knowledge are much more central than new equipment. A return to the general practitioner or family doctor requires the enhancement of their status, at the expense of hospitals. The same is true of the need to create a true nursing profession. All of this cannot be controlled by a new 'managerial' group, but requires social control. (Such social control is much better exercised at the local government level.) In the end, then, a successful health care system thrives best where there is democracy, greater equality, and an emphasis on education. Individuals do need to take personal responsibility for much of their health, but the vast body of new evidence underscores the social foundations of good health. Public responsibility thus enhances individual responsibility in health care.

Attention should be focused first on what kind of health care is needed. Once this debate is addressed properly, the question of how to fund that health care, and what can and should be afforded, makes sense. In terms of the efficient utilisation of given financial resources, there is no apparent advantage to social insurance or 'Bismarck' systems over the Swedish or British 'Beveridge' system of funding through taxation.

Whilst there are serious constraints on funding for these, middle-income, countries, the most important problem is in assuring the greater efficiency of the existing systems. A high-quality, high morale group of health professionals is central to this process. Attempting to 'managerialise' instead, for cost containment, is not a recipe for success. Within this framework, the development of a high quality nursing profession and a high standard and morale for family and general practitioners is critical. The concept of the professional nurse should be central to new developments in the hospital sector in particular.

The family or general practitioner can be an effective 'gatekeeper' to other medical services, and thus a good cost-controller. The use of doctors in this way to ration medical care, including pharmaceuticals, is never easy. It is, however, preferable to the situation where medical care costs do the rationing. In the case of ordinary drugs, rationing by price may not just be inequitable, but, by allowing the worsening of existing illnesses, will also be inefficient.

To continue to improve health services, adequate funding is necessary, no matter what efficiency gains can be realised. Given the general problems of tax compliance in the region, an 'hypothecated tax', collected expressly for health spending, makes a great deal of sense. Where new social insurance systems appear to perform this function of making payment less unpopular, and have been implemented successfully, energy is undoubtedly better spent on other aspects of reform. But in those countries where financing reform has not been successful to date, serious consideration must be given to maintaining a 'Beveridge' system, with hypothecated taxes supplying extra finance where this is clearly in line with the country's ability and desire to pay.

Housing

Contrary to popular perception there is no quantity crisis that demands the large-scale diversion of resources into housing construction at this point. What is critical is the maintenance and improvement of the existing housing stock. Energy-efficient retro-fitting is possible and likely to be an important step on the road to sustainable development. The legal barriers preventing this – such as the absence of good condominium legislation – can be as important as capital shortages.

So there is no need for financial resources to be diverted into 'jump-starting' a mortgage market at this time. The urge to engage in political bidding for the middle sectors of society – through mortgage support in particular – can establish long-term regressive structures for which there is no justification. Caution should also be exercised in rushing to a system of high 'market' rents sustained by housing allowances. This may deepen the poverty trap. Improvements in 'targeting' in this area may be especially damaging if they encourage further geographic segregation of differing social and income groups. A well-tapered system of allowances, and careful consideration for minimizing housing segregation must be part of the programme.

The major area needing attention is the mechanism for repair, the assessment of what is to be done with housing which it does not seem economic to repair, and the improvement of sound but unattractive housing, especially on large estates. This is critical, too, for the question of housing policy as part of integrated urban policy. In the longer run, with economic growth, housing will properly emerge as a major issue. By then, it is desirable for the legal and financial infrastructure to be in place. If social housing has not been reduced to 'dump estates', the prospects will be much brighter for an attractive package resembling the best west European experience.

Although there may be no overall crisis, there is a definite need to improve the capacity of young families to enter the housing market, and of the unemployed to move to where there are work opportunities. A good, if limited, social housing programme can fruitfully address these issues. It promises a higher return, and thus greater economic efficiency, than major programmes of housing benefit and higher rents, despite the promises made by their advocates.

Housing policy is, at the moment, much more of a damage limitation exercise. The damage that should be limited is both physical and social. Physically, it is the further decay of the inherited housing stock. Socially, it is pervasive and stubborn social exclusion resulting from the free working of the market mechanism in the housing area. This potential damage is one of the greatest threats to welfare in the transition countries. The social damage that can result from poor housing policies is – unfortunately – already widely visible in north

America and western Europe. The transition countries have the possibility of learning from this experience. The development of local government – which has already made good progress in central Europe – must play an important part in developing an effective and responsive housing policy.

Pensions

Clearly there is no 'ideal model' for pension reform. The debate in the west has focused predominantly on the perceived disadvantages of pay-as-you-go (PAYG) pensions as compared with fully-funded (FF) systems. Most of these disadvantages are illusions created by rather poor economic analysis. In fact, PAYG systems are typically cheaper to run, significantly more egalitarian, and obviate the need for additional 'safety-nets' for the elderly. But PAYG systems do have the disadvantage that they tend to be locked in to future pensions commitments that can, in circumstances of low growth or high unemployment and an ageing population, be unsustainable. Against the chequered background of pension reform attempts in different transition economies, however, the following course is the best approach for a country that has inherited a non-sustainable PAYG system.

First, the cost of pensions must be related to the rate of economic growth and to the demographic structure of the society by, where necessary, scaling down generosity towards pensioners in order to bring the system closer to sustainable levels, through reduced benefits (including loss of indexation, or indexation to prices rather than wages) and/or increased contributions and/or longer working life (also for the sake of inter-generational fairness, subject to social consensus). There should be direct, specific and transparent support of any part of the PAYG system which cannot be financed by contributions via government subsidies, as well as recapitalisation of outstanding implicit fiscal liabilities, at which point the PAYG system can remain in place as a solid and viable first pillar of the pensions system.

If there is a positive political assessment of the net advantages of a FF system, it should be introduced through thc transformation of that part of the old PAYG system which is not financed by contributions and has to be covered anyway by government subsidies, into individual accounts within the a new funded pension scheme (the so-called second pillar).

The government should also promote a third pillar of voluntary private savings, preferably with some tax-privileges in order to partially compensate for any initial scaling down of pension provisions with respect to the former PAYG.

Anti-poverty policies

Anti-poverty and inequality-reducing programmes are not purely an 'economic burden'. International experience shows that greater equality is positively associated with a wide range of social indicators and has discredited the 'Kuznets hypothesis'.

To raise revenue to finance social programmes it is important to widen the tax base. This involves a variety of measures aimed at reducing the relative size of the informal sector, reducing capital flight, and increasing taxes on real estate and consumer durables (eg cars and boats).

The inefficiencies of means-tested benefits suggest that an effective policy option is to restore the emphasis on universal child benefit/family allowances. Universal child benefits were introduced in western Europe when per capita GDP was not higher than that in eastern Europe now. The question is not affordability, but willingness to pay. The fact that children have been hardest hit by the transition is an unacceptable long-term risk. Moreover, the very low transactions costs of universal child benefit, make this one of the most cost effective ways of tackling poverty. Economies in child benefit are possible. Benefit could start at the second child. Or benefits could be integrated into the tax and benefit structure. The social solidarity and investment in human capital of child benefit is affordable. Means testing child benefits is a mistake. Where there are means-tested benefits, they should be designed so that each member of the household has an incentive to work. Employment-conditional benefits for families can be used to increase the in-work incomes of families.

In countries with significant Roma populations, protecting them from persecution and cooperating with Roma organisations to raise their incomes and provide them with jobs, medical care, education and transfer payments (where appropriate), must form part of effective anti-poverty programmes.

All social benefit changes should be transparent, and widely discussed. The specific impact on women of each measure should be considered automatically.

Even when policy is successful in creating employment, there will, nonetheless, remain the problem of specific groups of the population, for example the disabled. Although national programmes to meet their special needs are important, experience indicates that strong local government, together with non-governmental organisations, can be very effective in developing programmes to meet the special needs of such groups.

Concluding remarks

Any discussion about social policy and the welfare state is necessarily highly political. Whilst the emphasis of the argument above has been on the relationship between the welfare state and economic efficiency, it would be naïve to suggest that the question of the scale and content of social policy is purely 'technical'. The determination of what sort of society should be built in central and eastern Europe is up to the people of those countries – they have already made major political choices, and more need to be made. As far as social policy is concerned those choices should be informed by a mature economic consideration of the costs and benefits of the welfare state.

References

Arrow, KJ (1951) *Social Choice and Individual Values* 2nd edn, Cowles foundation, New Haven, 1963.

Balabanova. D (1995) 'Health care reforms in Bulgaria: Current problems and options for development' *Eurohealth* No 2 pp25-28.

Balchin, P ed (1996) *Housing Policy in Europe* Routledge, London.

Barr, N (1992) 'Economic theory and the welfare state: a survey and interpretation' *Journal of Economic Literature*.

Barr, N (1998) *The Economics of the Welfare State* 3rd edition, Oxford University Press, Oxford

Barro, R, and Lee, J-W (1994) 'Losers and winners in economic growth', in M Bruno and B Pleskovic, eds *Proceedings of the Annual Bank Conference on Development Economics 1993* World Bank Publications, Washington DC.

Benoit, B and Vipotnik, M (1997) 'Pension crisis spurs reforms in Eastern Europe' *The Financial Times* 19 August.

Bergson, A (1938) 'A reformulation of certain aspects of welfare economics' *Quarterly Journal of Economics* (Originally published under the name A Burk).

Blanchard, O (1997) *The Economics of Post-Communist Transition* Clarendon Press, Oxford.

Blanchflower, D and Oswald, A (1994) *The Wage Curve* MIT Press, Cambridge, Mass.

Blane, D, Brunner, E and Wilkinson, R eds (1996) *Health and Social Organization: Towards a Health Policy for the 21st Century* Routledge, London.

Boeri, T (1994) '"Transitional" unemployment' *Economics of Transition* vol 2 no 1.

Borooah, V (1988) 'Income distribution, consumption patterns, and economic outcomes in the UK' *Contributions to Political Economy*.

Buckley, RM and Gurenko, EN (1997) 'Housing and income distribution in Russia. Zhivago's legacy' *World Bank Research Observer* Volume 12 no 1.

Campbell, J and Owsiak, S (1994) *Fiscal Reforms in Post-Communist Countries* Krakow University Press, Krakow.

Chand, SK and Jaeger, A (1996) 'Aging populations and public pension schemes' *IMF Occasional Paper* 147, Washington, December.

Clarke, S (1998) Household survival in a non-monetary market economy (paper presented at a conference on *Barter in post-socialist economies* King's College, Cambridge, 13-14 December)

Clarke, S (1999) 'Poverty in Russia' in Stavrakis, P (ed) *Problems of Economic Transition* Sharpe, ME Armonk NY.

Commission on Social Justice (1994) *Social Justice: Strategies for National Renewal* Vintage, London.

Commander, S and Tolstopiatenko, A (1998) 'Unemployment, restructuring and inequality in transition' *mimeo* EBRD and World Bank.

Crooks, E (1989) *Alcohol Consumption and Taxation* IFS Report Series No 34, Institute for Fiscal Studies, London.

Danzinger, S, Haveman, R and Plotnick, R (1981) 'How income transfer programs affect work, savings and the income distribution' *Journal of Economic Literature* pp975-1028.

de Castello Blanco, M (1998) 'Pension reform in the Baltics, Russia, and other countries of the former Soviet Union' *IMF Working Paper* 98/11, Washington.

Eatwell, J (1994) 'The co-ordination of macroeconomic policy in the European Community' in Michie, J and Grieve Smith, J (eds) *Unemployment in Europe* Academic Press, London.

Eatwell, J (1997) 'Effective demand and disguised unemployment' in Michie, J and Grieve Smith, J (eds) *Employment and Economic Performance* Oxford University Press, Oxford.

Eatwell, J (1997) 'Pensions' *mimeo* Queens' College, Cambridge.

Eatwell J (1999) 'The anatomy of the pensions crisis' *Economic Survey of Europe* No 3 United Nations Economic Commission for Europe, Geneva.

Eatwell, J, Ellman, M, Karlsson, M, Nuti DM and Shapiro, J (1995) *Transformation and Integration: Shaping the Future of Central and Eastern Europe* IPPR, London.

Eatwell J, Ellman, M, Karlsson, M, Nuti, DM and Shapiro, J (1997) *Not 'Just Another Accession': The Political Economy of EU Enlargement to the East* IPPR, London.

Eatwell, J and Milgate, M (eds) (1983) *Keynes's Economics and the Theory of Value and Distribution* Duckworth, London.

Eatwell, J and Milgate, M (1995) 'Competition, prices, and market order' in Colonna, M and Hagemann, H (eds) *Money and Business Cycles, The Economics of FA Hayek, Volume One* E Elgar, London.

Economist *The World in 1998* London.

Elbirt, C (1997) 'Albania under the shadow of the pyramids' *Transition* The World Bank, Washington.

Ellman, M (1984) 'The crisis of the welfare state – the Dutch experience' in Boulding, K (ed) *The Economics of Human Betterment* Macmillan, London

Ellman, M (1994) 'The Increase in Death and Disease under "katastroika"' *Cambridge Journal of Economics*

Ellman, M (1997) 'Transformation as a Demographic Crisis' in S Zecchini (Editor) *Lessons from the Economic Transition* OECD/Kluwer, Dordrecht, Boston, London,

Elster, J, Offe, C and Preuss, U (1998) *Institutional Design in Post-Communist Societies* Cambridge University Press, Cambridge.

Esping-Andersen, G (ed) (1996) *Welfare States in Transition* Sage, London.

European Economy (1996) 'Broad economic guidelines' *European Economy* no 62 Brussels and Luxembourg, pp128-131.

European Bank for Reconstruction and Development (EBRD) (1997) *Transition Report 1997* London.

European Commission (EC) (1995) *Statistics on Housing in the European Union 1994* EU, Brussels and Luxembourg.

European Commission (EC) (1996a) *European Economy no 62, Broad Economic Guidelines* EU, Brussels and Luxembourg, pp128-131.

European Commission (EC) Directorate General for Economic and Financial Affairs (1996b) 'Pension reform in central Europe' in *European Economy* no 2, Supplement C, July.

Fazio, H and Riesco, M (1997) 'The Chilean pension fund associations' *The New Left Review*.

Feldstein, M (1974) 'Social security, induced retirement and aggregate capital formation' *Journal of Political Economy*.

Flemming, J (1998) 'Equitable economic transformation' in Tanzi, V and Chu, K-Y (eds) *Income Distribution and High-Quality Growth* The MIT Press, Cambridge Massachusetts, London.

Fisher, FM (1983) *Disequilibrium Foundations of Equilibrium Economics* CUP, Cambridge.

Freeman, R (1995) 'The limits of wage flexibility to curing unemployment' *Oxford Review of Economic Policy*.

Galbraith, JK (1992) *The Culture of Contentment* Houghton Mifflin, New York.

Garrison, C and Lee, F-Y (1992) 'Taxation, aggregate activity and growth' *Economic Inquiry*.

Giddens, A (1998) *The Third Way* Polity Press, Cambridge.

Glyn, A and Miliband, D (eds) (1994) *Paying for Inequality: The Economic Cost of Social Injustice* Rivers Oram Press, London.

Goetzman, W (1997) 'A century of global stock markets', *mimeo* Yale University.

Gordon, LA (1997) *Polozhenie naemnykh rabotnikov v rossii 90-x godov* Institute for World Economy & International Relations, Moscow.

Gregg, P and Manning, A (1997) 'Labour regulation and unemployment' in Snower, D and de la Dehesa, G (eds) *Unemployment Policy* CUP, Cambridge.

Ham, C (1997) *Health Care Reform: Learning from International Experience* Open University Press, Buckingham.

Haveman, R (1985) 'Does the welfare state increase welfare? Reflections on hidden negatives and observed positives' *De Economist* no 4.

Hedlund, S & Sundstrom, N (1996) 'The Russian economy after systemic change' *Europe-Asia Studies* vol 48 no 6.

Hegedus, J, Mark, H and Tosics, I (1996) 'Uncharted Territory: Hungarian Housing in Transition,' in Struyk, RJ (ed) *Economic Restructuring of the Former Soviet Bloc: The Case of Housing* Urban Institute Press, Washington DC.

Heidenheimer, AJ, Heclo, H and Adams, CT (1983) *Comparative Public Policy* Macmillan, London.

Hills, J (1991) *Untangling Housing Finance* CUP, Cambridge.

Howell, D, Duncan, M and Harrison, B (1998) 'Low wages in the US and high unemployment in Europe: a critical assessment of the conventional wisdom' *CEPA Working Paper Series I no 5*. Center for Economic Policy Analysis, New York.

Hsaio, WC (1995) 'Abnormal economics in the health sector' in Berman, P (ed) *Health Sector Reform in Developing Countries* Harvard University Press, Boston.

Hutton, W (1995) *The State We're In* Jonathan Cape, London.

Iglesias, E (1998) 'Income distribution and sustainable growth: a Latin American perspective' in Tanzi and Chu (1998).

Institute of Macroeconomic Analysis and Development (IMAD), (1997) *Slovenian Economic Mirror* December, vol III no 11, Ljubljana.

International Labour Office (ILO) (1996) *World Unemployment 1996/97: National Policies in a Global Context* ILO, Geneva.

Jaffee and Reynaud (1996) 'Developing a housing finance system in transition economies' *World Bank Policy Research Paper 1697* Washington DC.

Jönsson, B and Musgrove, P (1997) 'Government financing of health care' in Schieber, GJ (ed) *Innovations in Health Care Financing: Proceedings of a World Bank Conference, March 10-11, 1997* World Bank Discussion paper No 365, World Bank, Washington DC.

Kettle, DF (1993) *Sharing power. Public Governance and Private Markets* Brookings Institution, Washington, DC.

Keynes, JM (1936) *General Theory of Employment, Interest and Money* Macmillan, London.

Kitson, M and Michie, J (1994) 'Depression and recovery, lessons from the interwar period' in Michie, J and Grieve Smith, J (eds) *Unemployment in Europe* Academic Press, London.

Kleinknecht, A (1998) 'Is labour market flexibility harmful to innovation?' *Cambridge Journal of Economics* vol 22 no 3, May.

Kluve, J et al, (1999) 'Active labor market policies in Poland: human capital enhancement, stigmatization, or benefit churning?' *Journal of Comparative Economics* vol 27 no 1.

Kornai, J (1988) 'The borderline between the spheres of authority of the citizen and the state. Recommendations for the Hungarian health reform' *Collegium Budapest Discussion Paper* no 48, August.

Korpi, W (1985) 'Economic growth and the welfare state: leaky bucket or irrigation system?' *European Sociological Review*.

Kosals, L and Rykina, R (1998) *Sotsiologiya perekhoda k rynku v Rossii* Editorial URSS, Moscow.

Kreps, D (1990) *A Course in Microeconomic Theory* Princeton University Press Princeton, NJ.

Kucera, D (1998) 'Foreign trade and men and women's employment and earnings in Germany and Japan' CEPA *Working Paper Series I, no 9* Center for Economic Policy Analysis, New York.

Lackó, M (1999) 'Hidden economy – an unknown quantity? Comparative analysis of hidden economies in transition countries in 1989-1995' *Working Paper 9905* Institut für volkswirtschaftslehre, Johannes Kepler Universität Linz.

Laporte, B and Schweitzer, J (1994) 'Education and training' in Barr, N (ed) *Labor Markets and Social Policy in Central and Eastern Europe* Oxford University Press, New York, for the World Bank and LSE.

Le Grand, J and Robinson, R (1976) *The Economics of Social Problems* Macmillan, London (first edition).

Leimer, DR and Lesnoy, SD (1982) 'Social security and private saving: new time-series evidence' *Journal of Political Economy*.

Liebfritz, W, Roseveare, D, Fore, D and Wurzel, E (1995) *Ageing Populations, Pension Schemes and Government Budgets: How do they affect saving?* Paris: OECD Working Papers, vol III no 68.

Lindbeck, A (1998) *Lessons from Sweden for post-socialist countries* Collegium Budapest Institute for Advanced Study, Discussion Paper Series n 50, November.

Lindert, P (1996) 'Does social spending deter growth?' *Challenge* May/June.

Lubyova, M and van Ours, J (1999) 'Effects of active labor market programs on the transition rate from unemployment into regular jobs in the Slovak Republic' *Journal of Comparative Economics* vol 27, no 1.

Lukes, S (1999) 'The last word on the third way' *The Review* – The Journal of the Social Market Foundation March.

McCrone, G and Stephens, M (1995) *Housing Policy in Britain and Europe* UCL Press, London.

Mandic, S and Stanovnik, T (1996) 'Slovenia: fast privatization of the stock, slow reform of housing policy' in Struyk, RJ (ed) *Economic Restructuring of the Former Soviet Bloc: The Case of Housing* Urban Institute Press, Washington DC.

Maret, X and Schwartz, G (1994) 'Poland: social protection and the pension system during the transition' *International Social Security Review* no 2 pp51-69.

Marglin, S and Schor, J (eds) (1990) *The Golden Age of Capitalism* OUP, Oxford.

Marmor, TR (1994) *Understanding Health Care Reform* Yale University Press, New Haven.

Meslé, F (1996) 'Mortality in eastern and western Europe: a widening gap' in Coleman, D (ed) *Europe's Population in the 1990s* OUP, Oxford.

Meyers, RJ (1981) *Social Security* Irwin, Homewood Ill.

Michie, J and Grieve Smith, J (eds) (1995) *Managing the Global Economy* OUP, Oxford.

Micklewright, J (1999) 'Education, inequality and transition' *Economics of Transition* vol 7 no 2.

Milanovic, B (1996) *Income, Inequality and Poverty During the Transition* Research Paper series, no 11, World Bank, Washington, DC.

Mladenova, Z (1997) 'Country report: Bulgaria' in *EMERGO* – Journal of Transforming Economies and Societies vol 4 no 2, Spring, pp21-36.

Mooney, G (1994) *Key Issues in Health Economics* Harvester Wheatsheaf, New York.

Mortensen, J (1994) *Retirement Provision Now and in the Future* Brussels: Centre for European Policy Studies.

Mroz, T & Popkin, B (1997) *Monitoring Economic Conditions in the Russian Federation: the Russian Longitudinal Monitoring Survey* 1992-96 University of North Carolina, Chapel Hill, NC.

OECD (1981) *The Welfare State in Crisis* OECD, Paris

OECD (1990) *Health Care Systems in Transition: The Search for Efficiency* OECD Social Policy Studies No 7, Paris.

OECD (1994) *The OECD Jobs Study* OECD, Paris.

OECD (1996a) *Strategies for Housing and Social Integration in Cities* OECD, Paris.

OECD (1996b) *OECD Economic Surveys: The Slovak Republic* OECD, Paris.

OECD (1997) *Making Work Pay: Taxation, Benefits, Employment and Unemployment* OECD, Paris.

OECD (1998) *Reviews of National Policies for Education: Russian Federation* OECD, Paris.

Okolski, M (1985) 'The case of Poland' in Vallin, J and Lopez, A (eds) *Health Policy, Social Policy and Mortality Prospects* IUSSP, Liège.

Okun, A (1975) *Equality and Efficiency: The Big Tradeoff* The Brookings Institute, Washington, D.C.

O'Leary C, Kolodziejczyk, P and Lazar, G (1998) 'The net impact of active labour programmes in Hungary and Poland' *International Labour Review* vol 137 no 3.

Ours, JC and Ridder, G (1995) 'Job matching and job competition: are lower educated workers at the back of job queues?' *European Economic Review* vol 39, pp1717-1731.

Oxley, M and Smith, J (1996) *Housing Policy and Rented Housing in Europe* Chapman Hall, London.

Preker, AS and Herbert,WB (1995) 'Healing the wounds' in Paine, L (ed) *New World Health* Sterling, London.

Renaud, BM (1996) *Housing Finance in Transition Economies: The Early Years in Eastern Europe and the Former Soviet Union* Policy Research Working Paper 1565, World Bank, Washington.

Rimashevskaya, NM and Yakovleva, EN (1998) *Rossiya – 1997. Sotsial'no-demograficheskaya situatsiya* Institute for Socio-economic problems of the population, Moscow.

Roberti, P (1994) *Can Belarus Have a Sustainable and Cost-effective System of Social Protection Without Growth and Price Stability?* Fiscal Studies, World Bank.

Robinson, JV (1937) 'Disguised unemployment' in *Essays in the Theory of Employment* Macmillan, London.

Rosa, J-J (ed) (1982) *The World Crisis in Social Security* Institute for Contemporary Studies, San Francisco.

Rutkowski, M (1998) 'Overview of pension reform in transition economies' IIA Conference on *The Future of European Pensions* 26-27 February 1998, London.

Saltman, RB and Figueras, J (1997) *European Health Care Reform: Analysis of Current Strategies* World Health Organization. Regional Office for Europe, Copenhagen.

Seeth, H, Chachnov, S and Surinov, A (1998) 'Russian poverty: muddling through economic transition with garden plots' *World Development*.

Shapiro, J (1995) 'The Russian mortality crisis and its causes' in Åslund, A (ed) *Russian Economic Reform at Risk* Pinter, London.

Shapiro, J (1997) 'Health and health care policy' in White, S et al (eds) *Developments in Russian Politics* Macmillan, London.

Shimer, R (1998) 'Why is the US unemployment rate so much lower?' Bernanke, B and Rotenberg, J (eds) *NBER Macroeconomics Annual 1998* MIT Press, Cambridge Mass.

Shonfield, A (1965) *Modern Capitalism* OUP, Oxford.

Singh, A (1995) 'Pension reform, the stock market, capital formation and economic growth: a critical commentary on the World Bank's proposals' *mimeo* Cambridge.

Smith, DM (1989) *Urban Inequality under Socialism* Cambridge University Press, Cambridge.

Sobczak, A (1998) 'Universal health insurance in Poland: construction of the system and problems of its implementation' *Institute of Finance Working Papers* no 56, Warsaw.

Spulber, N (1997) *Redefining the State: Privatisation and Welfare Reform in Industrial and Transitional Economies* CUP, Cambridge.

Standing, G (1996) 'Social protection in central and eastern Europe: a tale of slipping anchors and torn safety nets' in Esping-Andersen (1996) *op cit.*

Struyk, R (1996) 'The long road to market' in Struyk, RJ (ed) *Economic Restructuring of the Former Soviet Bloc: The Case of Housing* Urban Institute Press, Washington DC.

Szelenyi, I (1972) 'Housing system and socialist structure' *The Sociological Review Monograph* vol XVII (February). Reprinted in *The Social Structure of Eastern Europe* Faber, BL (ed) Praeger, New York 1976.

Tanzi, V and Chu, K-Y (1998) *Income Distribution and High-Quality Growth* MIT Press, Cambridge and London.

Temin, P (1989) *Lessons from the Great Depression* MIT Press, Cambridge, Mass.

Terrell, K and Sorm, V (1999) 'Labor market policies and unemployment in the Czech Republic' *Journal of Comparative Economics* vol 27 no 1.

Turner, B (1996a) 'Sweden' in Balchin, P (ed) *Housing Policy in Europe* Routledge, London.

Turner, B and Victorin, A (1996) 'Housing policy in eastern Europe: the case of Estonia' in Struyk, RJ (ed) *Economic Restructuring of the Former Soviet Bloc: The Case of Housing* Urban Institute Press, Washington DC.

United Nations Development Programme (UNDP), (1997a) *Human Development under Transition: Europe & CIS* New York.

United Nations Development Programme (UNDP) (1997b) *The Shrinking State: Governance and Sustainable Human Development* New York.

United Nations Development Programme (UNDP) (1999) *Human Development Report for Central and Eastern Europe and the CIS* UNDP, New York.

United Nations Economic Commission for Europe (ECE) (1997) *Economic Bulletin for Europe* vol 9.

United Nations Economic Commission for Europe (ECE) (1997a) *Economic Survey of Europe, 1996/1997* United Nations, New York and Geneva.

United Nations Economic Commission for Europe (ECE) (1997b) *Trends in Europe and North America, 1996/97* United Nations, New York and Geneva.

United Nations Economic Commission for Europe (ECE) (1998a) *Economic Survey of Europe, no 1.*

United Nations Economic Commission for Europe (ECE) (1998b) *Economic Survey of Europe no 2.*

United Nations (UNICEF) (1995) *Poverty, Children and Policy: Responses for a Brighter Future* The MONEE Regional Monitoring Report no 3, Florence.

United Nations (UNICEF) (1997) *Children at Risk in Central and Eastern Europe: Perils and Promises* The MONEE Regional Monitoring Report no 4, Florence.

United Nations (UNICEF) (1998) *Education for All?* The MONEE Regional Monitoring Report no 5, Florence.

Visser, J and Hemerijck, A (1997) *'A Dutch Miracle': Job Growth, Welfare Reform and Corporatism in the Netherlands* Amsterdam University Press, Amsterdam

Vodopivec, M (1999) 'Does the Slovenian public works program increase participants' chances to find jobs?' *Journal of Comparative Economics* vol 27 no 1.

von Bredow, L (1995) 'The reform of health care in the Czech Republic' *Eurohealth* no 2 pp22-25.

Warner, AM (1997) 'The emerging banking system' *mimeo*, Harvard Institute for International Development, June.

Weisbrod, BA and Worthy, JC (1997) *The Urban Crisis. Linking Research to Action* Northwestern, Evanston.

Whitehead, C (1980) 'Fiscal aspects of housing' in Sandford, C Pond, C and Walker, R (eds) *Taxation and Social Policy* Heinemann, London.

Wilkinson, RG (1998) *Unhealthy Societies. The Afflictions of Inequality* Routledge, London.

Wood, AJB (1994) *North-South Trade, Employment and Inequality: Changing Fortunes in a Skill-Driven World* Clarendon Press, Oxford.

World Bank, (1991) *World Development Report 1991: The challenge of Development* Oxford University Press, New York, for the World Bank.

World Bank, (1993) *The East Asian Miracle* Oxford University Press, New York, for the World Bank.

World Bank (1994) *Averting the Old Age Crisis* OUP, Oxford.

World Bank (1996a) *From Plan to Market* Oxford University Press, New York, for the World Bank.

World Bank (1996b) *Russian Federation: Towards Medium-Term Viability* World Bank, Washington DC.

World Bank (1997) (Subbarao, K *et al*) *Safety Net Programs and Poverty Reduction: Lessons from Cross-Country Experience* World Bank, Washington DC.